Blessings In the Chaos

Tavia Bradford

Copyright © 2024 by Bold Publishing

Published by Tavia Bradford in Partnership with Bold Publishing
https://boldpublishings.com/

Book Layout by Opeyemi Ikuborije
Book Cover by Bold Publishing Tavia Bradford

Manufactured in the United States of America

ISBN: 979-8-9917255-0-7

Library of Congress Control Number: 2024921336

Follow Tavia Bradford

Social Media Outlets:

Instagram: @author_tavia.b
Linkedin: Tavia Bradford
Facebook: Tavia Bradford
Tiktok: @author.tavia.b

Contents

Dedication

To the world's okayest mom: Lisa Lynn

Ma, as a child, I failed to fully comprehend the depth of your love and the immense sacrifices you made for Boo and me. I was quick to criticize without understanding the selfless intentions behind your actions. However, as I blossomed into the woman I am today, I realized that every decision you made was driven by a steadfast desire to secure our well-being.

You have been an unwavering pillar of strength, never faltering in your support. I harbor an immense and profound love for you as our hearts are joined together and remain unbreakable. You have been rockin' with me the longest, Ma! The debt of gratitude I owe you can never be fully repaid, but I shall strive tirelessly to express my profound appreciation. Thank you for your boundless, unconditional love. I am truly blessed to call you my mom.

Foreword

We've all taken a journey filled with life lessons, lucky moments, dodged bullets, love, and loss, but rarely is it so eloquently yet authentically delivered. Tavia's journey traverses the landscape of tradition, tragedy, trauma, and triumph; creating a powerful narrative that resonates deeply with readers. This powerful body of work reaffirms our shared humanity, igniting inspiration and fostering resilience. It's a must-read for every woman who has questioned their purpose or path, wondered if her prayers are heard, or has asked the question, "When is MY blessing coming?" I wholeheartedly recommend savoring this book with a cup of herbal tea, allowing it to nourish your soul with sisterhood, unwavering faith, and dogged determination. Tavia superbly shows us that true strength lies not in avoiding life's blows or counting how often we fall, but in our capacity to rise time and time again. Her story serves as a beacon of hope, reminding us that our resilience defines us far more than our struggles.

-Lisa Nichols, Best Selling Author, CEO & Impact Speaker

Introduction

I often tell strangers my life story, and every time I do, they say I have a gift for storytelling and a remarkable journey worth putting down on paper or being on the big screen. I heard the camera adds ten pounds and I can't afford that. So here I am, trying my luck at this book thing.

For a long time, I brushed off the idea—me, write a book? Actually, if I'm being honest, I was being disobedient. I knew God told me to write this book. I would have never come up with this idea. I don't even like to read! Plus, writing papers was the hardest thing for me to do in school. I put it off for three years, but the suggestions to write kept coming from all corners, and I knew that was confirmation of what God had already told me to do.

In my book, you'll meet a girl transformed by unconditional love. Despite difficult circumstances, she has an unshakeable faith and knows she is blessed. Blessed, in the Greek, means "to speak well of" (biblehub.com/greek). God has spoken well of me. He has spoken immense kindness and grace over me. Even when I freak out at the slightest inconvenience, I remember my mother's words: "God's got you!" And she's right. Looking back, I realize there has never been a situation where I didn't come out on top. There have been plenty of challenges in my life. But in the end, God has always come through.

My life has been a tapestry of trials, triumphs, sorrows, and joys. With God's grace, I have emerged from hardship with resilience. In my weakest moments, when I strayed from the path, perseverance and faith saw me through. Though grief has carved life's valleys, extraordinary blessings crest each peak. This book presents a magnificent display of how God keeps His promises. He has never abandoned me, even when I didn't deserve His mercy.

I have a heart for those experiencing loss, especially mothers navigating the unfathomable depths of grief. Through the raw honesty of my experiences, I intend to build a sense of connection and community for others who feel alone in their grief. Although the journey is long, I aim to provide hope that joy can find you again. Stepping outside my comfort zone to write about this may be difficult, but I'm ready to be vulnerable if it helps even one person feel understood.

As you delve into my story, I invite you to contemplate your life's journey. Consider how each experience, whether exhilarating or challenging, has molded you into who you are today. Reflect on the enduring nature of blessings, which often reveal themselves even in the midst of chaos.

Chapter 1

Without My Permission: Letting Go Before You're Ready to Release

The day I found out I was pregnant, I was devastated. I remember thinking, *I can't even clean my room correctly. How am I going to take care of a baby?* My next thought was even more daunting—I'd have to call my ex. We hadn't spoken since our breakup. With shaking hands, I dialed his number.

"Hey," I said, trying to sound casual, "I'm pregnant."

"Okay, congratulations. But why are you telling me?" he said, sounding confused.

My best friend, Modesty, yanked the phone out of my hands and exclaimed:

"You know, good and well, she's not like that! And it's yours! You need to get over here now!"

"Give me a minute to process this. I'll head over as soon as I can," he said as he exhaled.

I let out the breath I had been holding. This wouldn't be easy, but I'd figure it out. I knew that I had to be pretty far along because my ex was the last person I had fornicated with. I'm just being honest y'all.

The next day, I went to the pregnancy resource center near work for an ultrasound. The nurse told me I was 4 1/2 months pregnant! I was shocked and mortified, and my only thought was that my grandma was going to kill me. Now, you're probably thinking: *How did she not know she was pregnant?!* Well, because I was on birth control, which clearly failed, and it made my periods irregular. The crazy part is, one week after finding out that I was pregnant, I also learned that I was having a boy. That completely changed the game for me. Not only was I going to be someone's mother, but I was going to be raising someone's future husband. That carried real weight with me. Sure, I'd be proud if my son grew up to be president. But more than that, I hoped his wife would tell me he turned out to be a good man and a loving partner. With so many lost men out there, I was determined not to contribute to that. This child deserved more.

The night before I went into labor, I stayed at my mom's house because I couldn't find parking where I lived and didn't feel like walking from Egypt to my apartment. Okay, obviously, I'm exaggerating, but that's how it felt at eight months pregnant. Zaire was active that night— moving so much it felt like backflips. I even had my mom feel my stomach, but of course, he stopped moving when she touched it.

"This boy's going to be just like you—doesn't like anyone touching him!" she joked.

The next day, I followed my routine, preparing for work as usual. However, I suddenly felt dizzy and weak upon arriving at the salon. I immediately tried to contact my doctor; she was unavailable so I had to leave a voicemail. Throughout the day, I began experiencing pain in my lower back. Assuming these were Braxton Hick's contractions, I decided to cancel my final appointment and return home to rest.

At home, I laid down with a heating pad for comfort. Unexpectedly, I felt a strong urge (attributed to Holy Spirit) to get up and use the bathroom. It was then that I discovered I was bleeding.

I immediately called my mom, who said to get to the ER—she thought I was in preterm labor. I told my ex, and he said he'd meet me at the hospital. When I arrived at the hospital, they rushed me up to labor and delivery, where I almost passed out. The contractions were so intense I was begging for relief. A nurse wheeled me in for an ultrasound, but they couldn't find my son's heartbeat.

"You're a little fluffy," the nurse said politely, "so we'll get a bigger machine."

The doctor tried again, then uttered the words that would haunt me forever: "Here is where the heartbeat should be. There is no heartbeat. He is dead."

Her tone was as dry as the Sahara Desert, and her eyes were cold as ice. Chhhhiiilllllleee, if I could have gotten up off that table, rage and agony would have consumed me, and she would have caught these hands (I wasn't all the way saved then). At that moment, my world collapsed. I felt like someone had ripped my heart out of my chest with their bare hands. I couldn't do anything but cry. I felt so helpless. My pregnancy had been smooth until now. This sudden tragedy was incomprehensible. I had never known death this intimately before, let alone the loss of my child.

Following Dr. Romero's devastating news that my son had passed away, I inquired about the possibility of a C-section. However, she advised that a vaginal delivery was the safest option for my health. Despite being on Pitocin for 12 hours, my labor failed to progress significantly, with only 1 cm of dilation. The prolonged retention of my deceased son in my womb led to complications. I developed an infection and began hemorrhaging. Due to these serious medical issues, the medical team had to monitor my condition closely, taking blood samples every hour.

The last blood draw indicated that my platelet count had dropped. The medical team warned that if this trend continued, I would need to be airlifted to a hospital in San Diego, as the current facility lacked the resources to manage such a critical situation.

Fearing for my life, I was convinced that being transferred via helicopter would be fatal. I urgently asked my friends and family to pray for an increase in my platelet count. Their prayers worked—my next blood test showed improved platelet levels. With this positive change in my condition, the medical team quickly prepared me for an emergency C-section.

As I was taken to the operating room, anxiety overwhelmed me, especially since hospital policy prevented any family members from accompanying me. Thank God, one of the nurses on duty that night was my best friend's cousin, providing a comforting presence. Adding to this unexpected comfort was the presence of Dr. Trujillo, the obstetrician I had initially hoped would deliver my son. Earlier in my pregnancy, she explained that she couldn't guarantee she'd be on call when I went into labor due to her practice's rotation system. These familiar faces offered some reassurance during this frightening and emotional time.

Before beginning the procedure, Dr. Trujillo informed me that I might feel some pressure but assured me I shouldn't experience any pain. When they asked about my comfort level, I deliberately reported feeling pain. My intention was to be put under general anesthesia, as I knew I couldn't bear the silence that would follow my son's delivery. The absence of his first cry was a reality I wasn't prepared to face.

Following my C-section, I was taken to the recovery room. During this time, without my knowledge, the hospital staff took my son to an upstairs room where my family had gathered. Each family member was allowed to hold Zaire and spend private time with him. By the time I was well enough to return to my hospital room, the nurses had already transferred Zaire to the hospital morgue. They planned to keep him there until I felt prepared to see him. I later learned that this is standard practice, as the cold temperature in the morgue slows down the natural process of tissue deterioration. This helps preserve the appearance of deceased infants, allowing bereaved parents to see their babies in the best possible condition when they're ready.

"Look, I don't want to see him if he looks crazy or his head falls off," I remember telling the nurse.

"None of that is going to happen, dear. It's okay if you're scared. I don't want you to leave here and regret not seeing your son," she replied in the most comforting tone.

So, I took her advice, and I saw him. He looked like a perfect sleeping baby; he only needed to open his little eyes.

The funny thing is, when I was pregnant, I would always say, "I hope my son doesn't look like his daddy or have my nose."

Well, guess what? He came out looking just like his daddy, and he had my nose. But at that moment, none of that mattered. He was mine, my son, my precious baby boy lying in my arms, lifeless, and there was nothing I could do or say to change it. I just wept and wept and wept.

I ended up falling asleep with him in my arms that night. When I woke up the following day, my son was still in my arms, and I freaked out. I remember screaming at the top of my lungs because of the realization that this wasn't a dream. My ex kept trying to console me, but to no avail. I was inconsolable. Imagine waking up to your deceased child in your arms. It was agonizing, and I didn't want it to be my reality.

Alarmed by my screaming, the nurse rushed in to see what was wrong. After I calmed down, I explained to her what was going on. She then told me the reason why they left Zaire in my arms. She informed me that it was against the hospital's policy to take the baby from me without my permission. At that moment, it didn't make sense to me, and I didn't care about any policy or procedures; I just wanted him away from me. It was far too much for me to bear. The medication's effects had faded, allowing the harsh reality of the situation to hit me like a ton of bricks.

During my C-section, I received three units of blood because I had been hemorrhaging. After receiving a transfusion, it is standard to administer saline to wash/salvage red cells blood and platelets. Since I had been on intravenous fluids for days, it began to swell me up. You could see every pore in my body. My feet were so swollen that it looked like my toenails were about to pop off.

In the midst of all this, I still had to begin the process of healing my body. That meant the nurses came in every couple of hours for me to get up and walk, which felt inhumane to me at the time. You mean to tell me that after just being cut open to deliver my deceased child, you want me to get up?! I just wanted to lay in the bed and cry.

I remember getting up to walk for the first time after surgery and feeling like there was something in between my legs. The only thing I could think of would have been the pillow I had my legs propped up on. So, I went to remove it, and it was just my thighs.

On my second night in the hospital, a nurse came to check on me, and to my surprise, I recognized her as the same nurse who had performed my ultrasound at the pregnancy resource center months earlier. She explained that while reviewing the patient list, she had noticed my name and came, hoping to see my baby. However, she quickly realized the tragic situation upon seeing the teddy bear on my door—a hospital symbol indicating infant loss.

Though I can't recall the nurse's name, her words are forever etched in my memory. She told me that God understands my pain because He, too, lost a son. She reminded me that I had given a perfect gift to God—my child went directly from my womb to heaven. Her words brought an immediate sense of peace, and at that moment, I experienced firsthand the comfort of the Holy Spirit.

The day before my hospital discharge, my family gathered for a bittersweet farewell to Zaire. We spent precious time creating lasting memories—taking numerous photographs, holding him close, praying together, and shedding countless tears. Faced with the impending reality of leaving the hospital without my son, I made the agonizing decision not to see Zaire on my actual discharge day. This choice, perhaps the most heart-wrenching of my life, was an attempt to shield my already fragile heart from further pain. I knew saying goodbye one final time might be more than I could bear.

In 2002, my friend had a stillborn, and to be honest, I thought it was strange that she had pictures of her child all around her house. But when it happened to me, I understood. That is your child, dead or alive, and that love doesn't cease just because they aren't alive. It makes you realize just how precious life is and how you should never take a day on this earth for granted.

Then there was the task of making arrangements for my son's body, which I was not mentally prepared for. Thank God for my grandparents, who took care of everything. One thing was for sure: I knew I did not want to have a funeral. I could not go through that. To me, it would have been like reliving the whole death of my son all over again.

Zaire's father and I decided that we would have him cremated. I couldn't even make any decisions regarding that, so I signed over my rights to my grandparents, and they took care of it. My grandmother chose a beautiful gold enameled box that didn't even look like an urn. I decided that it would be best for her to keep it at their house because I couldn't bear to look at my son's ashes every day.

When I was discharged from the hospital, the medical staff provided me with specific post-operative instructions. These included a two-week restriction on driving to ensure my safety and proper healing. They also advised me to avoid climbing stairs, as it could strain my incision site. And no hanky panky for six weeks. I also received guidance on how to suppress lactation, given that I wouldn't be breastfeeding. My doctor recommended an unconventional but reportedly effective method: using cabbage leaves. The natural compounds in cabbage help reduce milk production and alleviate engorgement. So, every day for a week, I placed cabbage leaves in my bra to suppress milk production.

Imagine having breastmilk and scars on your body from a child that you never got to nurture. It was a constant reminder of a devastating loss. These physical changes, typically associated with new motherhood and the joy of caring for a newborn, instead became symbols of my devastating loss. Each day, as I went through this routine, I was confronted with the stark reality of my situation—my body was prepared for a baby who was no longer there.

I found unexpected comfort in daily visits from my grandfather and Zaire's paternal grandfather. Their consistent presence became crucial as the house felt eerily quiet and empty, especially when others resumed their everyday lives. These two men made it their mission to ensure I wasn't alone in my grief. Their daily check-ins were a testament to their love and provided immense comfort. They didn't need to say much; their mere presence was comforting. We would sometimes sit in companionable silence, while other times, they'd share stories or simply listen as I expressed my feelings. Their unwavering support acted as an anchor during those initial days of loss, easing the transition from the intensity of the hospital stay to the challenges of everyday life.

During this period of profound grief and uncertainty, I found myself turning to my faith with renewed intensity. The depth of my pain, and my desperate search for meaning in this tragedy, led me to seek solace in my relationship with God. My spiritual connection deepened as I grappled with unanswerable questions and overwhelming emotions. This challenging time catalyzed my spiritual growth as I leaned on my faith for strength, comfort, and understanding in ways I never had before.

Once my doctor gave me the go-ahead to resume normal activities, I flew to New York for a three-week stay with my dad. This trip gave me the space to get away, clear my head, and properly grieve. During my visit, my dad took excellent care of me. He cooked homemade meals, went shopping with me, and listened attentively to my concerns. Sometimes, he simply let me cry on his shoulder when I couldn't express my feelings in words. We also, openly shared how my son's passing had strengthened our faith and drawn us closer to Jesus.

I always knew Jesus loved me; I learned that in church. However, it wasn't until I lost my son that I truly understood the depth of His love. As I worked on strengthening my relationship with God during this difficult time, I began to genuinely feel and appreciate His love for me.

I remember attending a Bible study where they had a guest speaker/ worship leader from South Africa, and before the Bible study started, they wanted to set the atmosphere so they led us in worship. It was the most intense and fantastic worship experience I've ever participated in. I remember just meditating on God's goodness, and suddenly, I heard this little voice say, "I love you, Mommy," and somehow, I instantly knew it was my son's voice. When I tell you, I was on the floor, I was on the floor! I was overwhelmed by God's grace and compassion for me. God knew I needed that because there were times when I would rack my brain trying to figure out why my son passed, and I even started to blame myself. Even though the doctors told me it was because of a placental abruption, they didn't know why it happened.

A few years later, I told that story to my friend's husband, who started crying, and he said it reminded him of how intimate God is and how He sets his affections on us. So, of course, I began to cry because I hadn't thought of it that way. It brought to mind the scripture where David said, "What is mankind that you are mindful of them, human beings that you care for them?" (Psalm 8:4, ESV Bible) As humans, we turn our backs on God, spit in His face, and deny Him daily. Yet He still loves us and wants nothing but the best for us. Okay, let me stop before I start preaching.

Every year, on my son's birthday, I do something to honor him. I believe that it also helps me to remember how blessed I am to have breath in my lungs still because I could have lost my life as well. They say time heals all wounds, but I don't think that's true because losing a child is something you never really get over. It hurts whenever I think about it, and I think about it often. I'd give anything to have my son with me, but I firmly believe everything happens for a reason. In unexpected ways, this pain has shaped me into who I am meant to be. This kind of trauma changes you. It etched away my naivety, giving me a stark but compassionate view of life. Now, I cherish every moment, taking nothing for granted because I know how fleeting it all can be.

"When my heart is overwhelmed,
lead me to the rock that is higher than I."
(Psalm 61:2b NKJV)

Chapter 2

The Genesis of the Blessings

You know that saying: God has a sense of humor? That is very accurate because I was born on April 1st. Yes, I, Tavia Nicole-Rene Gainer Jones Jackson, was born on April Fool's Day, and by the time you finish reading this book, you will say at least once that I'm a fool (silly). Oh, and don't you dare judge my name! It will all be explained. Just keep reading.

> ** Fun fact: April 1st, 1984, is also the day that Marvin Gaye was killed (my mom reminds me every year). He was shot twice by his father after he intervened in an argument between his parents. **

The day my mother left the hospital after giving birth to me is etched in her memory. As she waited outside for my father to bring the car around, an elderly white gentleman approached her and started a casual conversation.

"May I take a look?" he asked.

Though initially hesitant, my mother's instincts told her he meant no harm, so she obliged. He gazed down at me with a smile. Then, to my mother's surprise, he gently touched my tiny head.

"This is a blessed child!" he declared.

At first, my mom was taken aback because some strange man had just touched her child. But she knew, deep down, that this stranger had spoken truth over the life that had just begun. Whenever she tells this story, I get chills.

Just days after that blessing, death came knocking at my door. I napped while my mother relaxed in the living room with my grandparents. Suddenly, their cat began darting back and forth from the bedroom to the living room. My mom's motherly instincts kicked in, and she followed the cat to check on me. As she entered the room, a mother's worst nightmare unfolded before her eyes. I was gasping for air and turning blue. Fear and panic took over her body, and she began to scream and holler. My grandparents rushed in to see what was wrong. My mom's screams also caught the attention of our neighbor, who happened to be a registered nurse. The nurse ran over to our house and banged on the door. My grandfather let her in and led her to me. She instantly picked me up to see if there were any objects in my mouth. Then flipped me over to my stomach, and hit me on my back a couple of times. Suddenly, I could breathe, and everything was fine. The nurse told my mom that I had aspirated on formula. Things could have turned out very differently if it wasn't for that cat and the neighbor.

I find it extremely ironic that just days earlier, an elderly man spoke a blessing over my life, and now I was fighting for it. This incident wasn't just a close call; it was a testament to the power of the blessing. Every near miss and miracle since then has only reinforced that sense of being watched over and blessed.

Now, you may have to read this part more than once; whenever I tell this story, people often get confused. My family story is unique because I have three dads. You read that right, three dads! Let me break it down simply, my three dads are: Keith, my mom's high school sweetheart, David, who came into her life when Keith was away, and Jamie, who raised me as his own. Stick with me, and I'll explain how they each fit into my life.

Okay, so here we go. Lisa Lynn, AKA my mom, and Keith were high school sweethearts. They married after graduation, and Keith joined the army shortly after that. He was sent overseas to Germany and never called or wrote while he was gone so my mom thought, *He's probably out there doing his thing, so I'm about to do mine.*

She then met David and began to date him until Keith came home from Germany. Lisa Lynn decided that she was going to try to work it out with her husband, Keith. While Lisa Lynn was working it out, David was not having it. Long story short, my mom left Keith to get back with David, and she found out that she was pregnant. Mind you, this is 1984, so there was no DNA testing.

David said, "You've been with me more. It's my baby!"

I guess that logic worked for my mom, and they got married.

Over time, David became involved in a lifestyle that Lisa Lynn disapproved of. Realizing David wouldn't let her leave easily, she planned her escape. One day after work, she collected her paycheck, informed her boss she wouldn't return and left abruptly. Lisa Lynn then drove six hours to Oceanside, taking only me and the clothes on our backs.

A couple of weeks later, she returned to her former home with my grandpa to collect our belongings, and let's just say David was less than thrilled about this. He attempted to interfere and hinder my mom from gathering our stuff, but my grandfather stepped in, and David backed down. During this confrontation, Lisa Lynn told David he wasn't my father so he would leave us alone, and it worked.

Approximately a year later, when I was two years old, Lisa Lynn met a man named Jamie. They eventually married, and Jamie raised me as his own.

Y'all okay? Need a break? I know that's a lot to comprehend. My friends and family still get confused to this day. Whenever I tell a story and say dad/daddy, they ask, "Which one?" (so rude). So, to break it down: when I say "Dad", I'm either talking about Keith or David. It's all in the tone. When I say "Daddy", I'm talking about Jaime. Y'all got it?

Let's rewind a little bit. When my mom moved back to Oceanside, she introduced me to Keith and told him I was his daughter. Growing up, I knew that there was a possibility that either Keith or David could be my biological father. But we went with Keith as the biological father because he, my niece, and I all have the same birthmark. Plus, my mom said we have the same blood type. Again, the logic!

One final breakdown: Keith is a possible bio-dad, David is a possible bio-dad, and Jaime is a bonus dad.

I'll never forget telling this story to a friend. She said some people don't even know who their father is, or their father chooses not to be active in their lives, and here you are with three men fighting to be your father. Talk about being blessed!

I was absolutely a grandpa's girl. He affectionately called me his co-pilot because I accompanied him everywhere. Whether it was a significant outing or a quick trip to the mailbox, I insisted on going along. My grandfather had a gentle demeanor and a great sense of humor. I remember one evening, he picked me up from a Girl Scout meeting and started singing an old gospel song.

"Grandpa," I laughed, "why do you always sing songs about Jesus?"

"Because, Co-Pilot, He's the reason for everything," he said smiling.

His voice was smooth and rich, and that's probably the reason why I love chocolate men who can sing.

Everyone who knew my grandpa loved him. No one had anything bad to say about him. Well, my grandma Helen did, but I'll get to her in a second.

My grandfather was truly special to me. He was the only person who genuinely understood and appreciated me for who I was. He provided a perfect balance of affirmation, compliments, wise advice, and loving discipline. He was always there to listen; never judging but constantly correcting with love. It's likely, thanks to him, that I have such a strong sense of self-worth today.

One of his most admirable qualities was his unwavering faith. No matter the situation, my grandpa always guided me back to Jesus. His dedication to prayer was remarkable—he knelt every night to pray well into his 80s, stopping only when he was placed in hospice care. Even being on oxygen couldn't deter him from this practice. His faith was a cornerstone of his life, and it left a lasting impression on me. His example of devotion and humility continues to inspire me to this day.

Quality time was my grandpa's love language. We could spend hours together in comfortable silence. However, when I'd prepare to leave, he'd suddenly exclaim,

"You're leaving already?!"

"Sir, I've been here for hours, and you haven't said a word!", I'd respond.

He particularly enjoyed picking me up from elementary school on early dismissal days. Our routine included a trip to Taco Bell, where we'd sit and talk about our days, life, and faith. These moments were precious opportunities for us to connect and share our thoughts.

Now, Helen, on the other hand, was a piece of work. Some people even called her a "Hellcat," which gives you an idea of her fiery personality. She was a vibrant redbone woman, full of spirit. Despite her strong demeanor, she was the apple of my grandpa's eye. He affectionately called her "Fox," and it was clear he truly loved and adored her.

My grandma would get in her moods sometimes and give my grandpa hell. We would try to defend my grandpa, and he would say,

> "Hey! That's my wife, and she can talk to me however she wants to."

I would just sit there dumbfounded and think: *Well, if that's how you want to be spoken to.* Helen always said what was on her mind and didn't care who liked it or not. One thing is for sure: she always kept it real!

There was no doubt that my grandma loved her family deeply and would stand up for any of us without hesitation. Despite frequently giving my grandpa a hard time, she took exceptional care of him.

My grandparents, or as I affectionately called them, Grandpeeps, were the most important, influential, loving, and genuine people I have ever known. I could count on them for anything I ever needed in life. Not only did they teach me unforgettable life lessons, but they also introduced me to Jesus. They were the ones who made sure that I was in church every Sunday, during vacation bible school, and at any other youth event the church had. The Bible says,

> "Train up a child in the way he should go, and when he is old, he will not depart from it." (Proverbs 22:6, ESV)

I'm incredibly grateful they guided me to Jesus, even when I didn't want to listen. My faith is the foundation of my life, and I genuinely believe that without it, I wouldn't be here today.

Growing up, I was the outspoken, sassy, bossy, and ride-or-die friend. My mom and school teachers had to constantly remind me that I was not in charge. My mom would say, "I am the parent, and you cannot tell me what to do." One of my preschool assessments noted that I was a fast learner, and my favorite part about preschool was when they made me feel like the teacher. Oh, and I was not too fond of nap time. As I got older, my report card comments would say something like: "Tavia is a pleasure to have in class, but she talks too much and thinks she is the teacher."

In the second grade, my teachers noticed that I would finish my work early and then go around and disrupt the other students. They didn't think I was being challenged the way I needed to be, so my teachers recommended that I be tested for the Gifted and Talented Education (GATE) program. The term "gifted and talented student" refers to "children and youth who demonstrate higher performance capability in an intellectual, creative, artistic, or leadership capacity or in specific academic fields and who require services or activities not ordinarily provided by the schools to develop such capabilities fully." (nagc.org) I was accepted and began the program at the beginning of my third-grade year.

The GATE program was offered at Laurel Elementary, a magnet school across town. Magnet schools are public schools with enrichment programs designed to attract and serve specific targeted subgroups of potential students and their families. I went from attending a predominantly white school to a predominantly Hispanic school, which was a bit of a culture shock for me, but I loved every bit of it. I especially loved learning the language and visiting the candy lady on the same street as our school.

After school, a group of us would stroll down to the candy lady's house, where we'd indulge in treats like the tangy Pelon Pelo Rico tamarind candy, flavorful Sabores, and crispy Chicharrones de Harina. Just thinking about those goodies makes my mouth water. This is where my deep appreciation for Hispanic culture first took root.

I remained in the GATE program until the end of my fifth-grade year. I learned how to play the violin and the recorder, which is essentially a plastic flute, and my mom would cringe every time I had to practice because of the high-pitched sound it produced. I was taught American Sign Language, and I only remember the alphabet and part of a song called "Over the River and Through the Woods". We made houses for mealworms as they were used to teach us about life cycles.

Overall, I remember it as an incredible experience where I met some wonderful people. One standout was Mrs. Vicki, the school nurse at Laurel Elementary. I spent a lot of time in her office due to my frequent mishaps—whether it was swallowing a screw, falling off the monkey bars, or getting my foot caught on a backpack and falling out of the bus. My cousin even joked that she enjoyed attending school with me because she often got to go home early because of my accidents. Needless to say, Mrs. Vicki and I became pretty well-acquainted.

To my surprise, Mrs. Vicki was also the school nurse when I went to middle school. I would visit her office to say hi or bring my friends to meet her. When she met my best friend, Brittany, they instantly hit it off. We became so close that Mrs. Vicki took us to meet her son, who lived in a medical facility in Orange County, about 45 minutes away from Oceanside, where we lived. He had a condition called hydrocephalus, which is a neurological disorder caused by an abnormal buildup of cerebrospinal fluid in the ventricles (cavities) deep within the brain. This condition caused him to be confined to bed due to the dramatic swelling of his head. I recall Ms. Vicki telling us that his head circumference was 28 inches, which helps illustrate the severity of his condition.

Brittany and I immediately fell in love with him. As soon as we walked in, he lit up. We were excited to see him, and he was excited to see us. We spent the day eating, reading, and just keeping him company. At the end of the visit, Mrs. Vicki thanked us for being so kind and loving toward her son.

Middle school was where I truly embraced my social butterfly nature. I served as a peer mediator, was involved in the associated student body, continued playing the violin, and joined the step team.

In sixth grade, I met Stefan Louissant. He had light skin; almost white but not quite, with curly hair and light eyes. I was utterly obsessed with him, and that infatuation lasted until I became interested in someone else. Unfortunately, my feelings weren't reciprocated. Although he knew I liked him, he never took advantage of that. Instead, he became a great friend. When we were in eighth grade, the Associated Student Body (ASB) organized candy grams, and Stefan sent me one with a rose. Honey, I could have died and gone to heaven that day.

Middle school is also where I experienced my first death. His name was Joseph. He was a friendly, likable Samoan kid with the most beautiful smile ever. Joseph died due to heart complications. It seemed like the whole school attended his funeral. In Samoan culture, they kiss the face when they go around to view the body. I was a kid, so I followed suit and vividly remember how cold he felt.

High school was a whole new world, but I was still obsessed with Stefan. I quit the violin and took speech class instead because the orchestra wasn't cool in high school, or so I thought. I considered myself a "good Christian girl." I mean, I wasn't perfect, but I didn't get into any significant trouble, and I didn't drink or entertain drugs. Okay, I had one incident in middle school where I got caught stealing a lipliner pencil at a grocery store, but that was it. Don't judge me!

Since I had a GATE background, I was accepted into the Advanced Via Individual Determination (AVID) program, where one of my teachers recommended that I take Advanced Placement (AP) classes. AVID's mission was to close the opportunity gap by preparing all students for college and career readiness and success in a global society. They offered college-level classes at my high school, and if you passed the class, your grade would be bumped up one letter grade, and you would receive college credit. I wasn't trying to do all that because I had already decided to attend cosmetology school. I begged my mom not to enroll me in any of those classes. She didn't listen to me, and I had to take AP Comparative Politics. Yes, it was as boring as it sounds.

By junior year, I was a full-on party girl, and my new obsession was Jacob Smit. He was mixed; Japanese and Black, the finest thing my 16-year-old eyes had ever seen. Plus, he had some muscles because he was on the football team. Once again, he was aware of my obsession but was not the least bit interested.

I was chunky and eccentric, always embracing my unique style. I loved wearing my mom's vintage clothes from the 80s, and I covered myself in glitter—on my eyes, lips, hair; everywhere. Orange was my favorite color, so I wore it often. My prized possession was a pair of bright orange Dickies I found at the indoor swap meet, and I wore them at least once a week.

Loud, very outspoken, and hilarious, might I add, is how I would describe myself. The boys at my high school certainly didn't pay me any attention. It was always someone outside of my school.

One summer, Jay, visiting his aunt, came to my church. He was very aggressive, and I wasn't used to that. Jay was on me like white on rice and declared that I was his girlfriend, and I just went along with it. He was my first kiss. I remember going to the movies with him, and he kept trying to hold my hand and I kept hoping he wouldn't try to kiss me. Well, at the end of the date, Jay kissed me. I don't remember the details, so it must have either been traumatizing or not that great.

My parents were completely unaware of all the shenanigans I was up to. I'm talking about skipping school, parties with free-flowing alcohol, and Mary Jane. I was crossing the border into Mexico at 16 years old, partying like I was 25, and getting home just in time to make it to school the next day. Drag racing in stranger's cars and plenty of other dumb stuff: I did all of that regularly. My friends and I partied so hard that one of my friends had to be rushed to the hospital because he got alcohol poisoning and had to have his stomach pumped at 16! I did all this while working at a Christian bookstore and being a contestant in the Jr. Miss pageant. Boy, was I leading a double life.

During my senior year, I met Earnest Lamar Ellington, the Third. He had just moved into a house across the street from me, and since I was the unofficial welcome to the neighborhood greeter, I went right over and introduced myself to the entire family. I learned that they had just moved back to California from Washington. I also learned that his father would work for the same company as my father (Keith).

Earnest was a couple of years older than me and had this flair that I found very attractive. I know what you're thinking. There I go again, being obsessed with someone who wouldn't piss on me if I was on fire. Don't judge me! I got that saying from my grandma.

This time, it was different. It wasn't a sudden obsession. It was a gradual fondness because I found him to be intriguing. Earnest worked

23

at the local convenience store down the street from where we lived, so I would see him often. I made the mistake of telling my mom that I was into him. She took it upon herself to ask him if he had a girlfriend, and he responded with, "Sometimes." I know y'all, I should have run then, but I was young and inexperienced. My mom then began to ask him if he would like to be my prom date. Mind you, I was standing right there, and I was mortified! I wished I could have vanished at that very moment. I felt like I was going to pass out from the embarrassment. To my surprise, he agreed. But I had to play it cool and act like I didn't want him to take me. What was I supposed to do?! My mom just made me look desperate. So, I politely declined. Naturally, I avoided that store and him for the next few weeks.

One Friday night, I was going to my high school football game and needed to stop by the store (where Earnest worked) first and of course, he was working and the only cashier at the time. I gave myself a little pep talk and went in line to pay for my things. When it was my turn to check out, I greeted him, paid for my things, and then said bye. I quickly returned to my car and realized I had forgotten to ask for cash back. As I got ready to go back into the store, Earnest walked out, and I noticed he had some jamming sneakers on, so I complimented him on his sneakers, which turned into him asking where I was going. Ya girl looked good cause my friends and I were going to a party after the football game. I told him my plans, and after that, I casually mentioned that we should hang out, and he was down with that, so I asked him for his number. He put his number in my Nokia cellphone and baby, you couldn't tell me anything after that.

"Before I formed you in the womb, I knew you,
and before you were born I consecrated you;"
(Jeremiah 1:5, ESV Bible)

Chapter 3

Love, Loss, and Legacy: Navigating Life's Transitions

If the events of my first date with Earnest indicated how our relationship would go, then I should have ended the date within the first thirty minutes. According to my recollection, Earnest wanted to stop for cigars before a kickback at a friend's house. For those who didn't grow up in California in the 90s to early 2000s, a kickback is a group of friends getting together at someone's house in a party-like situation... without calling it a party.

As I backed out of the parking spot, I smashed my bumper on a pole. I should have called it a night then and there. Driving on, Earnest rolled down his window to smoke, and when he tried to roll it back up, it jammed. As I sped around a corner, he pushed on the window to try to get it back up, and the glass shattered into a million pieces. The red flags had flown right over my head. By some miracle, we didn't crash, though we probably left chaos in our wake.

Earnest and I dated on and off for five years before I got pregnant. During those five years, I graduated high school and cosmetology school, started working towards my associate's degree, and landed my first cosmetology job at Super Cuts.

When I became pregnant, Earnest and I were broken up after he cheated again—the last straw for me. Even pregnant, I stood firm that we were over. He came up with every reason in the world why we should get back together, and I politely reminded him that there was no rule stating that we had to be together just because I was pregnant.

Still, Earnest attended every prenatal appointment with me. He was by my side when we lost our son—from the emergency room to the C-section and recovery. In our grief, we decided to give our relationship another try; we were bonded by the trauma we had endured. Just three weeks after our devastating loss, we rashly decided to get married. Word of advice: Never make decisions when emotions are high.

Earnest and I married young. Grief-stricken after losing our son; we didn't want to lose each other. In hindsight, we were not ready for marriage. By the time we approached two years of marriage, we had already grown apart. While I was embracing faith and church, Earnest was withdrawing. Desperate to save our crumbling union, I delivered an ultimatum—join my church, or our marriage would end. Though reluctant, Earnest joined my church, hoping to preserve our troubled marriage. He had the nerve to tell the Pastor that he was joining because he didn't want me to divorce him… and the pastor said it from the pulpit! He called Earnest a smart man. Y'all, I thought, *I know this man didn't just put my business all in the street!* I was so embarrassed, but I kept it G!

Those two years after we lost our son were incredibly difficult for us as newlyweds. We were both grieving deeply but in different ways; without the emotional tools to support each other through the pain. I remember times when the grief would hit me suddenly, and I'd start crying. When Earnest asked why, I reacted angrily, thinking, *How could you not know why?*

There were times when he wouldn't get out of bed. Now I understand he was coping with depression in his own way; I didn't recognize the signs of depression back then. We were doing the best we could to navigate immense grief with our limited emotional intelligence at the time.

Losing our child changed us profoundly as individuals. I found solace by drawing closer to God while he struggled with depression. Though we cared for one another deeply, the different ways we were processing our grief made it difficult to move forward together. With time and perspective, I've come to see that neither of us was to blame. We were two hurting people doing our best to cope after tragedy. Though incredibly painful, ending our marriage was necessary for us to heal.

After mourning the loss of my son, I then had to mourn the end of my marriage. The secondary loss is one that few speak of or prepare you for. Seeking solace, I turned inward and nurtured my spiritual growth. I committed to doing the internal work of refinement and renewal because I wanted to connect more deeply with God and discover the woman that He created me to be. That period of introspection realigned me with my faith. I unearthed strengths I hadn't fully embraced before. Letting go of past versions of myself opened space to bloom into the person God knew I could become all along. I gained clarity about my divine purpose through prayer, study, and quiet contemplation. My growth journey continues, but drawing closer to God during that time gave me the foundation to build upon.

I also volunteered as a lay counselor at my local Birth Choice center. It provided free, confidential support services related to pregnancy, sexual health, reproductive loss, and parenting from a pro-life, Christian perspective. I see it as a compassionate alternative to Planned Parenthood. Counseling young women about their bodies and pregnancy options brought me great fulfillment during my healing journey. I believed God purposefully placed this role in my path, as the center was next to the salon where I worked. It was also part of the same pregnancy resource center I had visited when I first learned I was expecting my son. By giving back to other women there, I found hope after loss.

On the one-year anniversary of my son's passing, my mom and I wanted to do something meaningful to honor his memory. I was inspired while volunteering at Birth Choice, where they would release balloons to remember babies who had passed away. We decided to write heartfelt messages, place them in bottles, and release them into the ocean. At sunset, we went to the harbor at Oceanside beach and walked down the long jetty[1] that protruded into the waves. Imagine me walking on the jetty in a skort with my Coach bag and sandals. Don't judge me! Back then, I had to look cute all the time.

As we reached the end of the jetty, we paused, prayed, and shed some tears. Taking a deep breath of salty air, we gently released the bottles into the ocean. Apparently, we should have tossed them farther because they landed on the rocks and shattered. We swiftly turned around to leave, hoping no one had noticed. I said, *Lord, please forgive us. We weren't trying to kill any mammals, fish, or crustaceans.*

A lady sitting on the rocks greeted us warmly while returning to the car after releasing the bottles. Next to her was a younger woman, perhaps her daughter.

---

1. (A jetty is a long, narrow structure stretching from the shore into the water, protecting a coastline from the currents and tides.)

"How are you ladies doing this evening?" she asked.

"We're fine," we politely responded and continued.

"It's a beautiful sunset," she called after us.

Still wrapped in our grief, I murmured in agreement, hoping to avoid further conversation. But her kindness persisted, and she asked what brought us out here.

"We were doing a little memorial thing," I replied.

"Would it be alright if I prayed for you?" she asked gently.

My mom and I looked at each other, wondering why this lady wouldn't stop talking to us. Though normally hesitant about prayer from strangers, I was like, alright, we're here, so let's go for it. She started to pray for peace and healing, and then she began to describe, in detail, everything that happened to me and my son. I opened one eye and tried to get my mom's attention, but she was too busy praying as she should be.

I was shook at that point because I wondered how this lady knew these details. She was saying every thought I ever had and hadn't told anyone because sometimes I would blame myself for my son's passing.

She told me that it was not my fault, "God sees you. He hears you. He loves you."

She also said that I would know Holy Spirit as my comforter. By the end of the prayer, my mom and I were just looking at each other like, *Harpo, who this woman?!* (*The Color Purple* reference).

The woman then introduced us to her daughter, who appeared to be about my age. I noticed the mother seemed to be around my mother's age. After the introductions, she turned to me and said,

"You are blessed, and everything will be alright."

All I could manage was a silent nod. Her words left me stunned and speechless. I have never been speechless.

As my mom and I continued to walk back to the car in silence, I looked back toward where the two women were sitting, and they were gone. I told my mom to look, and she didn't see them either. They couldn't have jumped off the side of the jetty. Well, they could, but they would have fallen to their death. They couldn't have walked past us and made it that far because we still had at least half of the jetty to walk before we reached the sand on the beach. After the sand, there was the parking lot. So, there was absolutely no way they could have gotten past us. They had vanished into thin air. At that moment, my mom and I looked at each other, and I said,

"I think they were angels," she nodded in agreement.

Since that encounter, I now see interruptions as divine appointments. That evening on the jetty was no coincidence but a reminder of God's love for me.

Death has a funny way of reframing one's priorities; after my son passed, my mother felt a sense of urgency in uncovering the answers regarding my paternal ancestry. While searching on Facebook for one of my potential bio dads, David, she stumbled upon his son. When my mom told me about this discovery, the idea of this potential half-brother sparked an intense curiosity: who was he, did he know about me, did we share any similarities? After hearing about him, I eagerly jumped on Facebook, scouring his profile for clues. I closely examined his pictures and noticed some similarities in our features. This led me down an internet rabbit hole, hoping to find a picture of David himself. The only image I came across was a mugshot. I compared it side-by-side with my own photo, studying every detail intently. I concluded we didn't look alike, in fact, his son bore more resemblance to me than he did.

For reasons I can't recall, I was compelled to message David's son, Jr, to introduce myself. I don't remember exactly what I wrote, but I essentially said, *I'm not sure if you've heard of me, but I wanted to say hello.*

I was stunned when he replied, obviously aware of who I was. *Dad has told me all about you,* he said.

Now, y'all, I was confused because he referred to David as our dad. My mind raced, thinking, *Whoa, he sees me as a sister!* But I had doubts that we were actually related. I didn't have the heart to tell Jr. that David might not be my father. Jr. shared stories of visiting David on vacation (what my family calls going to prison) and expressed his feelings about David's absence during his childhood.

After we connected online, Jr. and I exchanged numbers and kept in occasional touch on social media. About a month later, he mentioned coming to Los Angeles and asked if I'd like to meet up. I said yes and planned a weekend trip also to see family in the area. But at the last minute, his plans changed, and we never met in person.

Tragically, just a couple of months later, Jr. passed away in a car accident. My heart sank, realizing he had left this world thinking we were brother and sister. Had we met, I would have been honest about my doubts.

A few years later, my mom was helping my grandpa get dressed when she felt a lump on his back. Concerned, she immediately took him to the emergency room. However, they could not perform a biopsy right away since he was unable to lie on his stomach due to his oxygen dependence and impaired breathing.

The ER doctor suspected cancer but said it would need to be confirmed through other means. They scheduled a CT scan and an MRI for the next day to investigate further. The scans revealed masses throughout his lungs that had metastasized. A localized biopsy on one chest lump provided the dreaded confirmation—stage 4 lung cancer.

I was in the hospital room when my grandpa's primary care physician of over ten years delivered the devastating news, with tears glistening in his eyes. He explained that the aggressive cancer left few treatment options. My grandpa calmly informed the doctor that he did not want treatment anyway. At 84 years old, he felt blessed by God to have lived this long.

Hearing those words, my knees buckled and I sobbed uncontrollably. I had to leave the room to pull myself together, unable to believe what I had heard. My hero, the most remarkable man I've ever known, was dying. Profound sadness and disbelief washed over me in crushing waves. Once I managed to compose myself, I returned to the room as the doctor explained that they would be sending my grandfather home on hospice care. Though heartbroken, I resolved to cherish every remaining moment with this man who meant so much to me.

My family was devastated to learn the cancer had progressed so far without any apparent symptoms. All we could do was make my grandfather comfortable as we came to terms with his bleak prognosis.

I visited my grandparents' house daily to help care for them and one afternoon, my grandfather called me to his side and directed me to retrieve his briefcase from the closet. Solemnly, he explained that inside were all the documents to handle his funeral arrangements after he passed and to take care of my grandma in his absence. I struggled to hold back tears as this loving, wise man prepared me for his inevitable departure. We sat holding hands in poignant silence, hearts heavy but overflowing with a lifetime of cherished memories.

Though the thought of losing him was unbearable, I respected his wishes and promised to carry out his requests to the letter as a final act of love and devotion for the grandfather I cherished. Receiving that briefcase felt like a heavy mantle—both an honor and a mournful burden. At that moment, though grief-stricken, I grew in gratitude and maturity, determined to make him proud.

The day he passed, two weeks after his diagnosis, most of his children and grandchildren had gathered to spend time with him. When everyone left, my aunt Cammy volunteered to stay overnight so my mother and I could rest after having been his primary caregivers for the past few weeks. I had just arrived home, showered, and changed into my pajamas when my aunt called with the devastating news that my grandfather had passed away.

At that moment, my world stopped. Gripped by shock and grief, I somehow managed to rush back to my grandparents' house in a daze. My grandma was right by his side, holding his hand and asking, "What have you done?" The sight of my grandpa's body overwhelmed me with sorrow, and I began to weep uncontrollably. In the midst of my profound grief, I had to summon every bit of strength to support my mom and grandma.

Grandma quietly directed me to the cabinet, and I understood her request for a shot of Hennessy. With shaking hands, I poured one for her and then a glass for myself, though I had abstained from drinking for years prior. The man who had anchored our family was gone, leaving a void too deep to bear. I found solace in knowing he was at peace with our Lord and Savior.

Fourteen months later, my grandma passed away at the age of 91. During those 14 months, my mom, sister who i affectionately call Boo, aunt AV, and I cared for her like my grandpa instructed. My mom, in particular, quit her job and moved in to provide round-the-clock care; determined to make Grandma's remaining time at home as comfortable as possible.

My grandma lived a full life filled with love. She was married to my grandpa, her soulmate, for over 50 beautiful years. When he passed away, she was heartbroken and lost her will to live. She developed heart issues and was placed in hospice care a year after my grandpa's passing. A week after beginning hospice care, she fell into a coma-like state. The hospice staff warned us to prepare for the end, estimating she had two weeks left. But a couple of days later, she suddenly awoke and said, "Damn, I'm still here?!" then demanded fried chicken, making us all laugh.

My grandma always wanted to look her best, even in her final days. The lady wore MAC NC 42 Studio Fix Foundation until the day she passed and this hideous shade of orange MAC Lipstick. Don't tell her I said that though.

Despite rapidly losing weight from illness, she'd joke, "Look how skinny I am. You're jealous, huh?!"

Her fun-loving spirit shone through, even while facing her own mortality. She would always tell me to fix her hair and to make sure she looked presentable for visitors, especially for Jamal, a young man who attended her church and had grown close to my grandma. He said she reminded him of his grandmother.

My family and I would gently joke that Jamal was her "boyfriend," though, in her changed mental state, part of her seemed to believe the idea. After her stroke in 2010, she developed aphasia and confusion, sometimes thinking she was still a young woman. Aphasia is a language disorder that affects your ability to communicate. It's most often caused by strokes in the left side of the brain that control speech and language. She would say things like, "The light is on the sleeve" and "Call people stupid, Lester." Don't ask me who Lester is because I have no idea.

When my grandma lost her ability to communicate after her stroke, I volunteered to move in with my grandparents to assist with their daily needs. A speech therapist came over a few times per week to help rebuild my grandma's speech, but it was an uphill battle. Though my grandma would listen politely during the sessions, she refused to do the assigned exercises independently afterward. The therapist explained that while my grandma knew what she wanted to say, her words came out jumbled when she tried to speak. Anytime she tried to form a sentence, and it sounded crazy, we would laugh. Curse words and calling on Jesus were some of the only phrases that remained clear in her speech. Eventually, she just started to write down what she wanted to say.

My grandma passed away peacefully at home, surrounded by loved ones, just days after celebrating her 91st birthday. This was four months after hospice had estimated she had two weeks left.

I remember when my mom called me at work, saying grandma's breathing had changed and she didn't have much time left. I rushed over to be by her side. When I arrived, my mom needed a quick shower, so I sat with Grandma and held her hand, watching each breath intently, not knowing which would be her last. Her breathing slowed and became irregular. In those final moments, I witnessed the gentle transition as she took her last breath. I confirmed she had passed when I could no longer see the pulse in her neck. I yelled to my mom, who was in the shower, that Grandma had passed and she began to wail.

Though it was a sorrowful moment, there was also a sense of blessing that she transitioned gently at home with her family after having one last birthday celebration with us all.

"Blessed are those who mourn, for they shall be comforted."
(Matthew 5:4, ESV Bible)

Chapter 4

A Few Good Men

In 2015, at 31 years old, I was living my best life—single, successful, and devoted to serving God. My business was thriving, allowing me to travel and complete my first mission trip to India. I felt like I was in my prime until an unexpected turn: my nephew, Papa, came to live with me.

Papa holds a special place in my heart. Born nearly a year after I lost my son, Papa felt like a gift, bringing new light into my life. Though I didn't give birth to him, I've loved guiding Papa through many firsts. I took him to his first day of school, first amusement park, first football game, first concert, and I gave him his first haircut. Being present for him helped heal my spirit.

Becoming Papa's primary caregiver when he was four years old was a major life transition. I went from total freedom to scheduling my days around a child—no more spontaneous late nights or trips without notice. My independent lifestyle changed drastically, but being there for Papa was my priority. He brought love and laughter into my home when

I least expected it, and that was far greater than any of the freedom I gave up. My life took a beautiful detour, and I wouldn't have changed a thing.

My schedule now revolved around drop-offs, pick-ups, homework, and Parent Teacher Association (PTA) meetings. Yes, I joined the PTA and became the secretary. They wanted me to be the president the following year, but that was way too much for me. My world now was shaped by ensuring Papa never went without—giving him the nurturing, stability, and opportunities to thrive that all children need.

One evening, as I washed dishes, I was suddenly overwhelmed with emotion. It dawned on me that though I never got to raise my son, God had blessed me with the chance to help raise Papa. Watching him grow up has been one of my life's greatest privileges.

The tears that night were of both grief and gratitude. My heart was shattered when I lost my son, but Papa's presence in my life mended my heart in beautiful, unexpected ways. The special bond we formed helped patch the hole left by my son's passing.

Now that Papa's a teenager, our relationship has hit some bumps, as many adolescent-parent bonds do. Though I love him dearly, I confess his mood swings and backtalk can make me fantasize about throat-punching him! If you have a teenager, then you know what I mean. If you do not, don't you dare judge me!

But I take a deep breath and remember my teenage years when I exasperated my poor mother. Underneath it all, he's still Titi's handsome boy.

As frustrating as it gets, I'm trying to offer Papa grace, guidance, and space to come into his own. Our closeness these past years allows me to trust that our connection remains, though it looks different now. The joy he's brought me far outweighs the throat-punchable moments.

I know the day will come when we laugh together about his teenage years. For now, I'll keep taking those deep breaths whenever he starts working my nerves.

Just as I was embracing my new role as guardian to my four-year-old nephew Papa, God decided to spice things up a little by introducing me to my biological father. As I mentioned in Chapter One, there were two potential candidates. Ultimately, DNA tests confirmed it was David. Understandably, the news didn't excite him when I made contact. Learning you have an adult child you didn't raise is complicated. While connecting with him gave me some answers, it also confronted me with difficult emotions.

An unexpected call changed everything. I had just proudly purchased my first car on my own—a Kia Optima. Soon after showing it off, a man phoned, claiming to be from the finance company. Now, in my head, I'm thinking, *Uh, holdup, playa, I put a down payment, and my credit was good enough.* He told me his name, Joel, and asked me if I knew who David was, and I said,

"Yes, that's the man on my birth certificate."

"Well, I'm his brother, and I believe you are my niece," he said.

I was stunned. Mind you, I was at my best friend's house, and she was in the background, telling me to put him on speaker so she could hear the conversation. Joel explained that he had a daughter who lived near me and that he could connect me with her if I would like. The whole time he was talking, I was thinking, *I can't wait to get off this phone to call my mom.* And I did just that. I briefed her on the call and jokingly said,

"Your heathen ways have caught up to you."

I told her she needed to call that man back and explain that we were unrelated.

Later, she shared their conversation with me. Joel simply wanted to connect, feeling he had already missed so much. He told her his mom had told him to find me because she knew I was David's daughter. My mom was honest that my paternity was uncertain, but Joel was open to building a relationship, even if the odds were only 50/50 that we were family.

After speaking with my mom about her call with Joel, I finally asked the question I'd never thought to raise:

"Who do you think my dad is?"

When she said "David," I was stunned she hadn't told me sooner.

After 32 years, it was time for me to speak directly with David. I asked Joel if he could connect me with David. Soon after, David called me, retelling the story of his relationship with my mom. He explained how she was married when they met and also how my mom told him I wasn't his. Understandably, he had been convinced that I wasn't his daughter. I told him I didn't fault anyone for the decisions they made in 1984. I just wanted to know if he was my biological father.

David was initially hesitant about taking a paternity test, he wanted to spend more time getting acquainted first. But our first conversation—the ease of our banter, the similarities in our personalities, left me reasonably certain that he was my biological father. I cried after that conversation; I felt like I'd found a missing puzzle piece. I wasn't looking for it, but God had put it together at just the right time.

I believe the timing of my connection with David was perfect, as it happened after I had done the necessary inner work and was emotionally ready for it. Still, building this relationship was incredibly challenging.

Seeing our similar personalities reflected back felt jarring at times. He would frustrate me in ways that made me realize I likely did the same to others.

God taught me unconditional love through my father. He knew he couldn't teach me through a romantic relationship because I would drop them in a minute if there were things I did not like or couldn't control. Yes, ya girl had (ok, still has sometimes) control issues.

Whenever we disagreed or he said something hurtful, my first reaction was to cut off contact.

"That's it, I'm never talking to him again!" I would say.

I made numerous attempts to connect with my father, but he couldn't meet even this simple desire for a relationship. Despite my frustration, a pattern emerged. The day after a disappointment, I'd sense a gentle prompting from God to reach out to my father again. At first, I resisted, thinking, *Why do I always have to be the bigger person?* But the Lord persisted, and I listened.

Over time, the Lord gave me empathy for my dad and helped me understand him better. After being incarcerated for 23 years, adjusting to everyday life wasn't easy for him. David had been in survival mode with no room for feelings or relationships, which wouldn't change overnight. He was more focused on himself than bonding with me. I didn't like it, but I understood. At the same time, his emotional distance hurt me. I realized he simply didn't know how to be a father.

The problem with David was that he wasn't used to anyone questioning him or being as witty, intelligent, or slick at the mouth as he was. My uncle joked that David had finally met his match in me. Despite the bumpy start, I continued to try to cultivate a relationship with him. I sent 32 Father's Day cards to symbolize all the ones he had missed. I made a scrapbook of my life so he could get to know his daughter. I even drove 9 hours just to visit him while he was on "vacation" again. But none of that made a difference.

Though my father and I are currently estranged, I hold no resentment in my heart. I believe that our relationship unfolded as it was meant to, and I will continue to keep my father in my prayers, wishing him happiness and peace. I gave my all to build and sustain our bond, but some things are beyond our control. I trust that God has a plan for our relationship, and I will always keep the door open should the circumstances ever change.

Before delving into the details about my other fathers, I just want to let y'all know that my mom had a type—light skin, light eyes, and curly hair. Unsurprisingly, I resemble all three of them. Despite the stark differences in their personalities, they share one commonality: yours truly. Now, let's begin with the story of Jaime.

Jaime, whom I affectionately call Daddy, is the most colorful one of the bunch. He entered my life when I was two years old and has raised me as his own ever since. Born and raised in New York, Jaime is the epitome of a true New Yorker—direct, no-nonsense, and unafraid to speak his mind, even if it comes across as blunt or impatient to others. People often say he sounds like Sylvester Stallone.

Jaime was also a Marine, embodying the Corps' reputation for a neat and precise appearance. Whether in uniform or civilian clothes, he always looks sharp and well-dressed; I even saw him mow the lawn in a white linen suit once.

I'm his firstborn, and he proudly declares that to anyone who'll listen. This man exudes such unwavering confidence in his fatherhood that he'd take a paternity test with absolute certainty that it would confirm that I am his.

As vibrant as they come, Jaime couldn't care less about conforming to anyone's expectations. He's Jaime through and through, unapologetically himself. It's no wonder I've inherited his spirited nature. He's the very reason behind my quick wit and persuasive manner. My mom often jokes that I could sell a used car to a used car salesman, and that's all thanks to Jaime's invaluable lessons in hustling. He firmly instilled in me the belief that where there's a will, there's a way—no obstacles or setbacks were too great.

He also taught me the importance of self-reliance, though he's the exception to that rule. My daddy ensures his girls lack nothing, toiling tirelessly to provide. Following his example, I've learned to navigate life with street smarts, a touch of cunning, and a healthy dose of humor—all traits I proudly attribute to him.

Here's a little story about him to help you understand how he operates. When I was around 16 or 17, I was talking to this guy—or so I thought. It turns out he had a whole other situation with a baby mom in the military, but that's another story for a different day. This fellow, let's call him Q, was a bit older than me, he was 23 years old, to be exact. There y'all go, judging again. I was young and naive.

I would hang out with him and watch him work on his car. Since I knew my daddy was very protective, and a tad crazy, I'd sneak across the street to his garage. One day, Q had his garage open, and that's when my daddy showed up with the dogs. They were trained killers if you let him tell it. Their names were Tyson and Princess. Tyson was a German Shepard, and Princess was a Rottweiler. My daddy let them off their leashes, and they cornered poor Q against the wall, growling aggressively, all while my daddy was giving him the third-degree. Embarrassed, I bolted out of the garage and nearly collided with my friend Terris. It turned out he was the one who had told my daddy where I was. Terris disapproved of me spending time alone with an older man. Even though I was angry that Terris snitched, I knew deep down he was just looking out for me.

I am also Keith's firstborn, and he has always treated me as such. Keith is remarkably composed, never raising his voice or displaying anger or sadness in my presence. He is very laid back with a hint of wittiness. Now, don't get it twisted. Just because I haven't seen my dad deviate from his character doesn't mean it hasn't happened—I've heard the stories. But I'm not one to gossip.

While my dad appears composed and emotionless to others, and even me at times, I know he loves me deeply. However, he rarely outwardly shows his emotions. It wasn't until my first mission trip to India that I truly realized how my dad expressed his feelings. The week before I left, he called me daily, providing updates on India's weather, political situation, and any other information he could find. This level of frequent communication was highly unusual for my dad.

The day before my departure, he even came to my workplace and watched me work for at least four hours. It was then that I recognized his underlying worry about his daughter traveling to a foreign country. I distinctly remember telling my mom how Dad's behavior during that time was unlike anything I had ever witnessed from him before—a level of care and concern I had never seen. Despite his reserved nature, I can affirm his unwavering presence during significant moments in my life, whether school events or surgeries.

He instilled in me the importance of a strong work ethic. He is one of the most diligent and tireless men I know. I certainly get my workaholic ways from him.

Thanks to Dad's example, I learned the meaning of hard work. That drive motivates me to work hard every day to achieve my goals.

I fondly remember my first trip to Las Vegas with Keith and my younger sister Symone. We stayed at Circus Circus, which was thrilling for my young self, though I remember the carpets smelling like vomit. It felt like 1000 degrees outside, and I joked that my shoes were melting into the pavement. I was relieved when we headed indoors to enjoy the air conditioning.

While in Las Vegas, my dad also took us to the Hoover Dam, where we took a tour and learned all about its history and operation.

We did all the fun, kid-friendly activities and got whatever we wanted. We weren't rich, but he sure made us feel like we were. That first visit sparked a lifelong love of the city we'd return to year after year, creating treasured memories with my dad.

The men in my life each have a special place in my heart, irreplaceable in their own right. Their individual expressions of love and support have helped shape me into the woman I am today. I firmly believe that God's plan is flawless, and in His wisdom, He saw fit to bless me with the presence of each of these remarkable individuals, knowing precisely the impact they would have on my life.

"The steps of a good man are ordered by the Lord,
and He delights in his way."
(Psalms 37:23, ESV Bible)

Chapter 5

Divine Appointments

While working at the salon one day, a vendor approached my coworker inquiring about makeup services for a colleague. Since my coworker couldn't take on the job, she passed the opportunity to me. The gig involved doing makeup for a conference. As makeup artistry was my passion, I eagerly accepted the offer.

When I arrived at the venue, I applied makeup to three individuals. Just as I was about to wrap up the last person, a woman walked in and said,

"I know y'all ain't getting y'all makeup done without me! Young lady, do you have time for one more?" She asked.

I assured her that I did and proceeded to apply her makeup. To my surprise, I later discovered that she was the CEO and founder of the company hosting the convention. After completing her look, she asked if I could return the following day and then daily for the remainder of the event.

When the conference ended, she approached me with an unexpected proposal: to accompany her on set, offering my makeup expertise whenever required. The request caught me off guard, as I had underestimated my skills at the time. While flattered, I found myself faced with a minor predicament—I was committed to a full-time job and had just accepted a part-time position at Total Beauty as a High-end Beauty Consultant. I decided to work there part-time because they offered medical, dental, and a 401k program that I desperately needed. After all, I was self-employed.

Regrettably, I had to inform her that I could only assist her during her San Diego or Los Angeles County visits. So, her assistant forwarded me her calendar for the year and inquired about my availability to provide my services on select dates.

As I scanned through her calendar, I was astonished. It was packed with multiple engagements each day, spanning across various continents, with barely any downtime in between. Intrigued, I decided to look her up online, and what I discovered left me speechless. She wasn't just anyone; she was one of the world's most sought-after motivational speakers, a New York Times best-selling author, and a prominent figure in the media. I'll be honest with y'all—I had no idea who she was. Motivational speeches weren't my thing, and I thought they were a bunch of hogwash until I delved into her world. Witnessing her unparalleled ability to guide individuals toward achieving seemingly impossible goals and unlocking their boundless potential left me utterly impressed, and I'm not easily impressed.

I had never collaborated with someone of her caliber before, and despite her celebrity status, she remained remarkably grounded. On set, she either cooked for the entire crew or arranged for lunch to be catered. Old-school hip-hop and R&B always created the ambiance, which was right up my alley. Her warmth and inclusivity made everyone feel like part of her extended family.

Being a part of her team for seven years was a fantastic experience. I had the privilege of doing her makeup for one of her book covers, a couple of talk shows, multiple magazine features, and more. As time passed, my role evolved beyond that of a makeup artist. I took on additional responsibilities as one of her hairstylists, a wardrobe consultant, and an integral executive team member. As an executive team member, I traveled with her to the Bahamas to assist in selecting a residence, where I organized her closet and makeup collection.

I had fantastic experiences, encountered extraordinary people, and ate good food. Most importantly, I gained a sister-friend for life who imparted priceless wisdom that will forever shape my personal growth. What began as a simple referral blossomed into a divine opportunity to showcase my talents on a grander scale; all because I seized the chance to go above and beyond for an unexpected client. I truly believe that God favored me because I hadn't been actively seeking this opportunity; instead, it was graciously placed in my path.

One of the perks of doing her makeup was being in her personal space for at least 45 minutes. Initially, I thought we were simply having casual conversations, but she always managed to sneak in profound life lessons. We would talk about everything from food to relationships.

During one of our talks, I vividly remember her telling me that I needed to be fluid, soft, and flexible. I thought I was already fluid and flexible. In hindsight, I was deceiving myself. As long as things were exactly how I wanted them, I could totally be flexible. Fluid, to me, meant going with the flow, and I'm not that type of girl. I needed structure to know which direction the current was flowing. Did the current have fish in it? If so, what kind of fish? Ya girl had questions. Soft? I ain't soft; I already knew that 'cause I'm a G! (G stands for gangster, in case y'all were wondering). She would subtly provide me with books on the subject and gently remind me that if I wished to be my best self and have the best chance at a lasting relationship with the opposite sex, I would need to develop those attributes. Those 45-minute sessions were a sacred exchange; a mutual offering of time, trust, and guidance that would forever enrich my life's journey. God always knows what you need and when you need it. He knew I needed her wisdom and expertise during that time to prepare me for the next season of my life.

For nearly eight years, I remained single and focused on my relationship with Jesus. I had nothing to do with the male species whatsoever, until one fateful day in 2018. While visiting a church, I noticed a chocolate arm, seemingly illuminated by a celestial spotlight. Don't even judge me! I promise you it was like God had intentionally drawn my attention to him.

From that day on, our paths continued to cross unexpectedly. He even popped up in the "People you may know" suggestions on my Facebook page., Catrese a.k.a. Boo, saw it as a sign and urged me to message him, but I couldn't bring myself to do it because I believed he would have made it known if he were interested.

My family and I visited a local soul food restaurant one Sunday after church. To my surprise, I spotted him dining with a woman I recognized from my gym. My first assumption was that they were a couple, so I hesitated to approach them. However, Catrese advised me not to jump to conclusions and encouraged me to inquire about the situation.

Fate intervened, and the woman and I found ourselves together in the restroom. I politely asked the woman if they were a couple. She clarified they were just friends. Again, Catrese interpreted this as a sign and encouraged me to message him when we got home, but I reiterated that he likely wasn't interested. Undeterred, she argued that perhaps he was simply shy and issued an ultimatum—either I reach out to him, or she would take matters into her own hands.

It took me five days to muster the courage to send him a direct message on Facebook. To my recollection, I said something along the lines of: *Fancy running into you the other day. If I'm not being too forward, would you like to grab a bite to eat or coffee sometime?*

My heart raced with anticipation and uncertainty as I waited for his response, compulsively checking my messages every ten minutes. After what felt like an eternity, he finally replied, *It was indeed a pleasant surprise seeing you, and I'd love to get together for a bite to eat.*

We exchanged numbers and texted for about two weeks before graduating to our first phone conversation. The conversation flowed easily; before we knew it, nearly two hours had passed as we shared our life stories. As we prepared to hang up, he remarked with a hint of surprise that he rarely divulged so much to someone he barely knew. I laughed, explaining I had that effect on people. With an unmistakable chemistry brewing between us, we eagerly scheduled a late lunch date for two days later. Shout out to my sister for pushing me to contact him.

On my first date with Bryce, I was like issa husband! He had so many qualities I admired—namely, his faith, humor, love for football, no kids, good credit, and 401k. Did I mention he was chocolate and could sing? Ain't nothing like a chocolate, singing man! I could tell he was a responsible, family-oriented man, as well.

Our date unfolded into an entire day of shared experiences. We lingered at the restaurant for a delightful four hours, and to my surprise, he suggested we run an errand together. Following the errand, we went to Cold Stone Creamery for ice cream. From my perspective, the date couldn't have been more perfect. Chile, I was ready to say "I do", even though it was our first date! I didn't want to scare him off by coming on too strong, but I was definitely smitten.

Rather than rushing to vocalize my budding emotions, I chose to document this unfolding connection through the intimacy of my journal because I felt that our blossoming relationship promised captivating stories worth memorializing.

On our second date, we went to the movies. Although the specific details of the movie escape my memory, I distinctly recall finding it less than impressive, prompting me to sprinkle our conversation with a dash of sarcasm. It spices things up a bit.

In case y'all haven't caught on, I speak my mind. However, my candid demeanor may have been a tad overwhelming, as he went radio silent for two days following our outing. Sensing a shift, I took the initiative and inquired about his well-being. His response threw me for a loop. He stated he was fine but then accused me of being pushy and ungrateful. Hold up now! Pushy? Maybe. But ungrateful?! Never! I asked why he considered me ungrateful, and his response was so ludicrous that I burst out laughing, thankfully, it was over text and not in his face. According to him, the grave offense was my failure to express gratitude after he treated me to dinner and a movie.

After my laughter subsided, a sobering thought crossed my mind: *Who hurt you?* Without filter, I texted him the question. Unsurprisingly, he deflected with *I'm not hurt,* but I could sense he was.

For this relationship to bloom, it was evident that it would demand a significant investment of both patience and time on my part. Those close to me knew both my patience and my time were in short supply, yet for him, I had time. That day, I decided I would love him so deeply and so well that he'd forget his heart was ever broken in the first place.

After our last encounter, an uncomfortable silence lingered between us for three long weeks. Meanwhile, my 34th birthday was right around the corner, and I had plans to celebrate it with a dear friend in Japan.

For ten remarkable days, I explored ancient castles, strolled through serene gardens, and savored the excellent flavors of Japanese cuisine. Yet, despite the wonders that surrounded me, Bryce was still on my mind. When I had mentioned my travel plans before my departure, he expressed an interest in visiting Japan someday. With this in mind, I brought him souvenirs to share my experience with him. I prepared a delectable goodie bag comprised of popular Japanese snacks.

The day I returned home, I wasted no time texting Bryce to tell him about the goodie bag. To my surprise, he asked if he could swing by my place after work to pick it up. *Of course,* I responded.

As he approached my doorstep, my heart raced with a mix of anticipation and apprehension, uncertain of how this visit would unfold. I stepped outside to greet him, gave him a warm embrace, and presented him with the bag of Japanese treats. He expressed his heartfelt gratitude and genuine appreciation for my thoughtfulness.

We discussed the whole movie situation and decided to put that behind us and start fresh. Candidly, I expressed my need for consistent communication and to see him every day. Yes, I said every day. He lived 7 minutes away from me and had to drive past my house on his way home from work. So, I didn't see why he couldn't see each other everyday.

"You buggin'! Every day?!" he questioned; his tone a mix of amusement and skepticism.

"Yup, every day," I affirmed, my resolve unwavering.

"You're going to get tired of me."

"Trust me, I won't." My conviction remained steadfast.

From that day forward, we saw each other at least four times a week.

Bryce made me feel like I had found the man I was meant to be with. As stated, ya girl was ready to meet him at the altar in my white dress—cue Jagged Edge. But Bryce wanted to take the relationship slow and really get to know each other before making long-term plans. At first, I'll confess, I was slightly offended when he didn't fall in love with me after three business days. Like, hello, sir?! You have hit the jackpot and you're over here fumbling the bag!

I recall mentioning to him a piece of wisdom from my pastor: "Just as an employer can gauge a new hire's fit within 90 days, we should be able to discern within 30 days whether we're compatible for a relationship. After all, in matters of the heart, our intimacy surpasses any professional acquaintance's." That made sense to me, so what are we moving at a snail's pace for? I like you, you like me, and we go together! That was not his thought process at all. He wanted to just go with the flow. Again, I am not a go-with-the-flow type of girl. I'm a Holy Spirit-led woman!

Our relationship blossomed for a couple of months, bringing us closer each day. I knew I wanted to get him something special as his birthday approached. During one of our mall outings, he had admired a pair of dress shoes but ultimately decided against purchasing them. Seizing the opportunity, I returned to the mall and picked up the shoes, a tie set, and cologne that perfectly complemented the shoes he had eyed. I could hardly wait to see the look on his face when he unwrapped his presents.

My love language is quality time, but I naturally express love through thoughtful gestures and gift-giving as well. For Bryce, this was an entirely new experience. When I presented him with the carefully selected gift, he seemed taken aback, asking,

"Why are you so good to me?"

"What kind of women have you dealt with?" I replied.

His question hinted at past encounters where gifts came with ulterior motives or strings attached. I reassured him,

"This is simply a part of who I am. When I care about

someone, I enjoy finding ways to make them feel appreciated without any hidden agenda. I come from a place of genuine affection and sincerity."

It was evident that my thoughtful gesture had touched him in a way he hadn't experienced before, and I was determined to show him that love could be expressed freely without expectations or conditions.

A few months later, I had to travel out of town to help my goddaughter settle into her first year of college. Coincidentally, this trip overlapped with Papa's birthday, marking the first time I would miss it. Without prompting, Bryce took it upon himself to visit my house, bearing gifts for Papa—a box of his favorite candies, a t-shirt, and a heartfelt card with money inside. Despite my physical absence, he presented the gifts as if they were coming from me. When I learned of this selfless gesture, my heart swelled with profound gratitude and affection. That act of thoughtfulness solidified what I had already known—that Bryce was a rare gem, someone who understood the importance of cherished bonds and was willing to go above and beyond to honor them, even in my absence.

I immediately called Bryce to convey my heartfelt appreciation. As our conversation ended, I found myself on the precipice of uttering those three powerful words—I love you. The sentiment had been brewing within me for quite some time, a realization I had penned in my journal exactly a month into our courtship. These were my words:

God, I think this is it! I think this is him! Lord, please don't let me mess this up. I like him, and for the first time in forever, I am ready and willing to love unconditionally. Lord, show me how to be who he needs me to be and help me not to self-sabotage. Show me how to support, honor, and love him correctly. Mold me into the woman and wife you would have me to be. Give me the patience to be patient with him. Help me to love him through his hurt. Teach me to extend grace where he needs it. Help me to exhale and live in each moment that we have together. Don't overthink this, Tavia. It's going to take work and effort. This is what you prayed for, and God, thank you because I can sense that he will be more than I imagined. God help him to trust me with his heart. I promise I won't break it. I want to protect it and help him put every broken piece back to show him I will be gentle with it. I come in peace, love, and encouragement. Help me to show and model that. Lord, I want to see that beautiful smile for as long as you allow. Thank you, Jesus! Thank you.

The connection I felt with Bryce was unlike anything I had experienced before, surpassing even the bond I once shared with my ex-husband. This relationship felt like a precious gift from God. I was ready to let go of any lingering apprehensions and fully immerse myself in the journey. With an open heart and a renewed sense of wonder, I stepped forth, eager to embrace the adventures and growth that awaited, secure in the knowledge that this extraordinary love was a gift to be cherished and nurtured, no matter what challenges might arise.

"Listen to advice and accept instruction
that you may gain wisdom in the future."

(Proverbs 19:20, ESV Bible)

Chapter 6

Mac & Cheese: The Real MVP

After several months of dating, I felt it was time for Bryce to meet some of my friends. The perfect occasion arose when my C.E.O client, turned friend, hosted an engagement party for her son.

We arrived at the party a little early. I went upstairs to help my friend with her makeup while Bryce stayed downstairs. When I finally came downstairs, I found Bryce well-acquainted with the group, seamlessly fitting into their camaraderie as if he'd known them for years.

We ended up seated at a table with my friend's grandmother, Ms. B, or as we lovingly called her, Grandma B. She took an instant liking to Bryce's warm presence. With attentive chivalry, he ensured her plate was full and kept her laughing throughout the day. All the while, he never failed to remind me of how breathtakingly gorgeous I looked. Grandma B leaned over and whispered that it was plain to see how much he adored me. When she said that, I instantly got goosebumps because I had prayed for a man who would adore me.

By the end of the day, Bryce had thoroughly impressed my friend with the thoughtful care he showed her grandmother. She pulled him aside to express her gratitude and spilled a little tea about conversations we'd previously had regarding him. Before she overshared, I interrupted and told him it was time to go. My friend laughed and said, "One day, I'll fill you in completely."

After Bryce dropped me off at my car, he texted me. He admitted that he had lost count of how many times he wanted to kiss me during the evening. I replied frankly, *but you didn't kiss me.* To my surprise, he responded and said, *I'm on my way.*

Suddenly, I felt a rush of nervousness and excitement. I had been hoping for our first kiss for a long time, and now it seemed like it was about to happen. The realization left me flustered and a bit overwhelmed.

The anticipation built as I heard his car pull up. I took a deep breath and hopped out of mine. Our eyes met, and we kissed. It was beautiful, like a scene straight out of a romantic movie—the music swelling, the world around us faded away until there was just him and me and that perfect moment. In case you haven't noticed, ya girl fell hard. It's more like I face planted into the deepest pool of love.

A month later, one of my childhood friends threw a birthday party for her husband at a jazz lounge. I figured it would be the perfect opportunity for Bryce to meet the friends I grew up with.

When we arrived, the ambiance was alive with the smooth sounds of a live R&B band. Bryce and I joined my best friend and her significant other at a cozy table, where conversation flowed effortlessly over drinks and a shared meal. Everyone enjoyed themselves to the fullest that night, especially the band's captivating performance, which drew us to the dance floor several times.

On the drive home, we reminisced about the evening's delightful moments and how much we enjoyed each other's company. I confessed that I didn't want the night to end, feeling like I was riding a wave of pure euphoria. It had been the best evening yet with Bryce, and I felt myself falling deeper and deeper for him with each passing day.

The following day, I woke up feeling like the previous night had been all a dream, but the soft buzz of my phone dispelled that notion. I received a text from Bryce that made my heart flutter. He reiterated how wonderful the evening had been and how much he appreciated and adored me. Y'all, I melted just reading it. The lyrics of Bob Marley played in my head. "Is this love? Is this love? Is this love, is this love, that I'm feeling?!" Grinning from ear to ear, I texted *Ditto* and reminded him to request a half-day off from work for our upcoming date.

I purchased tickets to see one of my favorite artists, Anita Baker, in concert the following Friday. The thought of experiencing the soulful songstress's smooth, velvety vocals while wrapped in the arms of my heart's desire was exhilarating!

The time came to see the one and only Mrs. Anita Baker. On the morning of the concert, Bryce told me he wasn't going. He explained that he had a lot going on and had just received bad news about a fellow marine, so he needed some alone time. I was disappointed that we wouldn't see Anita together, but I understood.

I ended up taking my goddaughter to the concert, and boy, did we have a time! Even though she was a little too young to know any of the songs, she enjoyed watching me sing my heart out to every song.

Two days later, Bryce texted me and said he needed space to heal. He realized that he was bleeding on me, and I wasn't the one who cut him. I asked him to come and say goodbye to me face to face. He obliged. My journal entry for that day read:

> It's been six months, and it's over. You need space to heal. Let's hope you actually do that. Long story short, I asked you to come over and say goodbye. You came, we hugged, and I cried. You said

I am an amazing woman. I told you I loved you, I cried, and we kissed—the end.

Devastated was an understatement. I was down bad y'all. My mom and best friend were seriously worried about me falling into depression because they had never seen me so emotionally affected by a man. I was so hurt I couldn't even go to work the next day. He had the nerve to text me that morning and ask how I was doing. *Sir, what?! I'm a mess!* And that's when my hurt turned into anger. I politely told him about himself. Y'all, I read him left, right, up and down. I questioned his mental stability because breaking up with someone one day and then wishing them a great day the next makes no sense. I told him that although he had been hurt, he needed to take accountability for his actions instead of continuing to play the victim role because he caused emotional wreckage, too.

Weeks drifted by, yet the heartache still lingered. I swore off dating and threw myself the biggest pity party ever. I didn't take the breakup well because I always got what I wanted, and things always worked out in my favor. I was very emotional because I knew, beyond a shadow of a doubt, that God told me that Bryce was the one. When that reality crumbled, I felt betrayed, crying out:

Is this how you're going to do me, God?! I have served you and dedicated my life to you, and you just dangled my heart's desire in front of me and then snatched it away!

At that moment, I knew how Moses felt when God told him he would not enter the promised land. Oh, and by the way, I am very impatient, so when God told me Bryce was the one, I thought our story would unfold like a fairy tale love story, and boy was I wrong.

A month later, I ran into Bryce at the gym. Y'all, he walked right past me. To myself I thought, *Oh no, he didn't!* Naturally, I approached him at the massage chairs and asked,

"Are you really going to pretend you didn't see me?", with a slight attitude.

"I didn't see you."

His words and tone were distant. This was not the Bryce I fell in love with. I explained that I understood his desire for space to work on himself was not about me. However, I couldn't help but take it personally when he treated me like a complete stranger, seemingly carrying on with his life just fine, while I was left an emotional wreck. After that, I got up and left because he clearly didn't want to discuss it any further at the gym.

I continued to journal my thoughts and feelings as it was therapeutic for me. My journal entry the day after our gym discussion read:

Day 14 without you: You texted me this morning and said 'I owe you an apology for any disrespect that I have shown you. You are a phenomenal woman who deserves to be treated as such, and I have failed to do that. I will not disrespect you with vile words, actions, or emotions anymore. You deserve better, and I am ashamed of my actions.' Again, I questioned his mental stability. It took me a while to respond because I wasn't sure how to take it or how to respond. After contemplating what to say, I told him, 'All I ever wanted to do was love and care for you. But for some reason, you find that hard to believe. So, I've come to the harsh reality that this is where it ends. Thank you for apologizing, but you don't have to be ashamed. I still think you're amazing, even though there are some things I may not like or understand. My feelings have not changed. I have been my authentic self, but you don't seem to want it, and that's where I'm stuck.'

Of course, he didn't respond to my text message. However, we crossed paths once more at the gym that night. We ended up at the massage chairs again, and I asked why he hadn't responded to my text. Bryce's response was dismissive, claiming he was perhaps contemplating, just as I was. His pettiness sent me into an internal frenzy, but I had to contain myself since we were in public. Exasperated, I threw my hands up and said, "You win! I give up! Goodbye, Bryce."

With that, I turned and left. This emotional rollercoaster was too overwhelming for me. The constant ups and downs, the dizzying twists and turns of emotions, drained me of all my energy and stability. For my own sanity and peace of mind, I couldn't continue subjecting myself to this merciless emotional roller coaster.

After the breakup, I went rogue. I didn't totally walk away from the Lord; I knew better than that. I just indulged for a bit. I do not recommend it. It was very ghetto with a capital G! I gave it one star instead of zero because I did have a little fun. I'm just being honest, y'all.

A friend of mine has a friend who is a member of a phenomenal old-school, funk, and R&B cover band. The name of the band is Brothers Igniting a Groove (B.I.G). This was right up my alley because I love this type of music. I was instantly hooked the first time she took me to see them. Anytime B.I.G had a gig in San Diego County, we were there. Sometimes, we'd even road trip out of town to watch them perform.

With that whole concert scene came the drinking culture. Don't get me wrong, I enjoy a good libation occasionally, but this was a bit excessive. I would drink before we arrived, aka pre-game, drink when I arrived, and then continue to drink during the concert. It was never just one or two drinks.

Oh, and remember when I swore off dating? I lied. A few months after the breakup, I entertained several gentlemen, nothing serious or crazy, though, because my heart was still with Bryce. So, while I put on a front like I had moved on and put myself out there again, it was just surface-level stuff. No matter how many new fellas I hung out with, Bryce had me caught up in a whole other kind of way. My feelings for him were stuck on repeat in my mind and heart.

Even after our breakup, Bryce remained in my heart. God would instruct me to pray for him and to be H.O.T. (Honest, Open, and Transparent), in the words of Pastor Mike Todd, I didn't want to because there was still some hurt there. Yet, whenever I saw or heard about him, a voice in the back of my mind would whisper, *That's still my baby!*

Over the course of a year, Bryce and I engaged in a handful of conversations. The Lord's gentle nudge prompted me to reach out to Bryce each time. Remarkably, whenever I did, he would express sentiments like, "You always seem to contact me at the right time or say things that confirm what the Lord had revealed to me."

During that pivotal year, I elevated my part-time position at Total Beauty into a full-time job as an Elite stylist at the in-house salon. The management team had persistently tried to get me into the salon from the moment I began working there. Initially, I had reservations that the transition might compromise the financial stability I had grown accustomed to. Plus, I was unwilling to let go of the freedom to make my own schedule. However, my boss assured me that if I met the established goals as an Elite Stylist, I could pretty much do as I pleased. Challenge accepted!

My first corporate job at Total Beauty introduced me to the wonderful world of full benefits. The paid time off (PTO) was by far the best perk. Getting paid for vacations was a fantastic feeling I hadn't experienced before. Total Beauty's generous PTO policy allowed me to accumulate days off rather quickly. Plus, I started accruing the PTO even when I was a part-time employee and never used it. So, after transitioning to a full-time role, I had already banked enough time to take a two-week vacation just three months into my new position. I was thoroughly enjoying the perks of the corporate salon life.

Eight months into my full-time position at Total Beauty, the COVID-19 pandemic struck. Initially, many people underestimated the severity of this global outbreak caused by the novel Coronavirus. However, as the death toll rose and hospitals became overwhelmed with infected patients, the gravity of the situation became apparent. Ultimately, the entire country had to shut down, with only "essential workers" in sectors like grocery stores, healthcare, delivery services, some retail establishments, and agriculture were allowed to continue working.

This was a devastating blow to the cosmetology industry. People resorted to underground operations to get their nails and hair done illegally. When I say people, I mean me. I see those judgy eyes! I never thought I'd see the day when covert operations were necessary just to get a haircut. Thank God I transitioned to Total Beauty just in time. They kept a significant portion of their employees on payroll, ensuring our benefits and PTO continued accumulating despite being unable to work. I didn't miss a single paycheck during the shutdowns. God is good y'all!

The pandemic prompted me to start therapy, as I realized I needed an outlet. Before the world shut down, I was accustomed to a relentless work ethic, ripping and running, and the constant busyness of everyday life. However, when everything came to a halt, I went into a depression and experienced anxiety. I was one of those people who thought anxiety and panic attacks were not real until I had one myself in the parking lot of my job. I found myself ugly-crying for no apparent reason. I called my mom (because that's what I do), and when she asked what was wrong, I told her I didn't know and thought I needed to speak with someone professionally. A dear friend had recently started therapy and explained how immensely it had helped her, so I decided to give it a try.

Ok, y'all, I come from a Black Baptist family. So, therapy wasn't a thing. We just prayed and talked to the Pastor, and that was it. Thank God I now know it takes Jesus and therapy if you want to be free! Let me stop before I get to preaching.

Therapy was such a blessing as it allowed me to delve deeply into understanding what makes me tick. I've always prided myself on being self-aware, knowing the ins and outs of my being—the good, the bad, and the ugly. I had specific patterns I wanted to decode. I sought to understand why I reacted to situations in particular ways, why I felt the need to maintain control, and why I struggled with vulnerability, especially in relationships. I tended to swiftly move on if things didn't align with my expectations or if people didn't behave as I envisioned and I hoped to gain insight into these key areas through self-reflection and analysis.

Two years later, I prayed for Bryce as I often did, and the Lord instructed me to call him, but I hesitated. Yes, I actually told the Lord no— definitely not something I recommend doing. After trying to negotiate with God, suggesting I could send a text instead, He reminded me that He had specifically said to call him. So, I gave him a call, and he revealed that he had experienced a health scare. Once again, Bryce remarked how I always seemed to reach out at the right moment. Our conversation lasted for nearly an hour, and he filled me in on the details of his situation. We also engaged in some lighthearted banter before wrapping up. I felt fulfilled after following through with what God told me to do.

A few weeks later, I was on the phone with Bryce again. I can't quite recall who initiated the call, but I vividly remember being in the midst of preparing my delectable macaroni and cheese. He asked what I was doing and I said, "Cooking."

Curiosity piqued, "What are you cooking?" he asked.

"Mac and cheese," I said proudly.

His response was immediate and enthusiastic, "Your mac and cheese sounds delicious right about now."

Seizing the opportunity, I extended an invitation, "Well, why don't you come over and have some?"

Needing no further convincing, he eagerly accepted and said he would arrive within the next fifteen minutes.

The silence was awkward as we ate our mac and cheese. Which was rudely interrupted when my mother said, "Hey, stranger!"

I immediately went into prayer and braced myself for whatever might come out of her mouth next. Bryce rose from his seat, exuding southern charm as he warmly embraced her. My ever-inquisitive mother then asked him if this visit was a one-time deal or if we would see more of him. He responded with a courteous grin, "I don't know, that's up to Tavia."

So there I was, in this weirdly familiar but awkward situation, thanks to my mom's blunt question hanging in the air. She put me on the spot to decide if I wanted to rekindle things.

On the one hand, I was lowkey excited at the possibility, but on the other, my guard was up due to the previous hurt. My brain was short-circuiting, trying to figure out if he was sincere or just being polite to my mom. I really wanted him to be sincere because, despite everything, he was who I wanted.

After taking a deep breath to prepare myself mentally, I went for it.

"I would love that," I told him, praying this was the right decision.

"Love bears all things, believes all things, hopes all things,
endures all things. Love never ends."
(1 Corinthians 13:8, ESV Bible)

Chapter 7

We Wrestle Not Against Flesh and Blood

As the pandemic subsided and businesses reopened, I was thrilled to return to work. This might seem strange to some, but I loved my job and enjoyed my clients.

During the pandemic, some businesses allowed their employees to work remotely. While certain companies realized they could reduce overhead by permanently adopting remote work, others completely transformed or eliminated certain positions.

The company I worked for revamped its management structure, replacing the traditional salon manager role and introducing a new services manager (SM) position.

The new services manager role combined the responsibilities of the previous salon manager and prestige manager positions into one comprehensive role. The duties involved overseeing both the salon operations and the high-end beauty counters. However, a catch accompanied this restructuring—service managers could not actively work behind the chair as stylists. This meant the existing salon manager would have to relinquish their client book and focus solely on managing the team, overseeing the operations, and ensuring the smooth running of the business. The existing salon manager wasn't willing to give up being behind the chair, a decision that was entirely understandable given the personal investment in their craft and their client relationships.

To complement the services manager position, the company also created an assistant services manager (ASM) role, which allowed a stylist to remain behind the chair while contributing to the management duties. This hybrid arrangement perfectly aligned with my interests and aspirations. The ability to seamlessly balance hands-on client work with managerial responsibilities was right up my alley.

When I joined the salon team, my ambition was clear—to secure a management position within a year. Although the COVID-19 pandemic temporarily derailed that timeline, I was still determined to reach that goal. When the ASM opportunity emerged, I announced the position would be mine in front of the entire salon staff. This bold statement ruffled a few feathers because I was still considered a newbie.

Yet, I remained undeterred, making it clear that my priorities were achieving financial success and climbing the corporate ladder; but it was a bonus if I made friends along the way.

Fortunately, I did manage to cultivate a few cherished friendships, one of which blossomed into a particularly close bond. We regularly shared lunch breaks, exchanged hairstyling services, and assisted one another with clients. We even celebrated each other's birthdays with thoughtful gifts, embodying the camaraderie of "work besties." During the pandemic, I even prepared my famous macaroni and cheese and delivered it to her home as a gesture of kindness.

After the company filled the services manager position, our general manager (GM) visited the salon to announce that the ASM role was open and inquired if anyone was interested in applying. I eagerly stepped forward, expressing my interest and asking what steps I should take to apply. Notably, I was the sole individual who voiced an interest in the position when the announcement was made. The GM then invited me into his office to outline the requirements. He also informed me that he would consult the previous GM and district manager to seek their perspectives regarding my suitability for the role. That did not concern me, as I was confident in their positive regard for my work, having consistently exceeded expectations through my commitment to under-promise and over-deliver.

It just so happened that our district manager popped into our store for a surprise visit that day. This allowed my manager to discuss the possibility of me taking on the ASM role with her. After their little chat, they asked me to join them in the office. The district manager expressed that she considered me well-suited for the ASM position and mentioned having heard positive feedback about my work ethic and seen evidence of my performance in the store's metrics.

A few days later, my general manager informed me that he had spoken with the previous general manager, and she agreed that I would be an excellent fit for the assistant services position. He told me that the job was essentially mine, but I still needed to complete the formal application process. I then used the work computer to complete all the required paperwork.

I was elated, as this opportunity aligned perfectly with my professional aspirations, and the realization of my hard work was finally within reach.

Later that week, the services manager and retail manager called me into their office. Surprisingly, they informed me that someone else wanted to interview for the same position I was basically a shoo-in for. This person was upset that she wasn't given the opportunity to apply before they essentially told me I would get the job. They explained they also had to allow her to apply for the position to avoid a complaint to human resources (HR). I was okay with this because I knew I was better qualified, no shade.

The managers advised me that this person had spoken negatively about me behind my back and had attempted to throw me under the bus. They couldn't disclose the details of what was said for confidentiality reasons, but they revealed that it was the girl I had become close with at work. The managers advised me to be cautious in my interactions with her as she was not a genuine friend.

I was blindsided, hurt, and felt betrayed; mainly because we were the only African American women in the salon. We were supposed to stick together, not fight against one another. She could have come to me first, and I would have reassured her that we were friends, that this wasn't a competition, and that we could help each other. But after I received that information, my mentality shifted to "may the best woman win."

After leaving the office, the entire atmosphere of the salon had shifted. It was evident that they had been talking about me, and most of them seemed distant and unfriendly. I was furious but had to maintain a professional demeanor until I secured the ASM title. I knew she intended to throw me off my game, get under my skin, and provoke a reaction from me, but I refused to give her that satisfaction. All I can say is that she was very fortunate I had found my faith because the old me would have clocked out of work, asked her to meet me in the parking lot, and I would have knocked her head clean off her shoulders without hesitation.

From that point on, she gave me nothing but attitude and caused me constant frustration. The situation escalated to the point where even my clients noticed her hostile behavior towards me.

She turned most of the stylists against me, and some even threatened to quit if I became the ASM. While I understood it stemmed from jealousy, it still hurt my feelings. I loved my job and wanted the salon team to thrive. I knew I could lead effectively and cultivate success within the team. I was determined not to let any of them see that I was hurt. I continued performing my duties diligently and tried not to let the negativity affect me.

Finally, after waiting two months, I received the exciting news that I had been named the new assistant salon manager! I was excited and ready to take our services team to the next level. But guess who was salty? Yup, ol' girl. The very next day, she tried to undermine my authority and go over my head.

One of the stylists needed assistance with a hair color formulation. I guided her on what to do and then returned to my client. When I returned to check on the stylist, Miss Salty Pants told her to disregard my instructions and follow her way instead. I was livid! She was trying to make it seem like I didn't know what I was doing, and she was also doing this in front of the client. While she wanted to make herself look better, she failed to realize that this made the salon look unprofessional and incompetent.

I had to regain my composure, and I explained to her that was not the proper way to handle things. If she disagreed with my formulation, she should have pulled me and the other stylist aside to discuss it privately. She rolled her eyes and walked away, going to speak with the GM.

Thankfully, I had a great management team that supported me and told her that my instructions should be followed as the ASM unless they contradicted company policy. Boy, did that get her panties in a bunch, but I was glad to have the backing of the management team.

Miss Salty Pants was so upset that my GM didn't take her side she called HR the next day and told them that the management team was mistreating her. I had barely held the ASM position for two minutes before she started throwing temper tantrums.

HR had our GM conduct a mediation session between us. She stated that she felt we were plotting against her and trying to get her fired. Our GM assured her that was not the case and explained that she could not keep having these outbursts and undermining me, or it would affect her job. I remained cool, calm, and collected. I stated that I wanted to see the whole team succeed and that we are better when we work together. However, that meeting accomplished nothing because she still gave me an attitude the next day and did not speak to me. Despite trying to resolve the issues through the proper channels, Miss Salty Pants continued her unprofessional behavior.

As the new ASM, I had to start enforcing company policies that had previously been neglected. Many of the stylists didn't like that. I tried not to come in "with guns blazing" because I knew that would only ramp up the resistance. So, I introduced one new policy at a time.

The first policy I implemented was the daily appointment sheet. Before starting their shifts, the stylists were required to provide the manager on duty, a.k.a me, with an overview of their scheduled appointments for the day and their strategy to achieve their sales goals. Now, being the nice person that I am, I took it upon myself to print out their daily appointment sheets every morning. I would write each stylist's sales goals on their sheets and place them at their stations. This way, all they had to do was pick up their sheet and review it with me verbally. Miss Salty Pants found this extremely aggravating because she despised communicating with me.

I also had to modify some of the stylists' schedules to meet the needs of the business. This did not go over well at all. One stylist, let's call her Salty Jr., who had previously threatened to quit if I became ASM, actually followed through. She informed the services manager, my direct supervisor, that she intended to quit. The SM instructed her to submit her resignation in writing. Salty Jr. grabbed a piece of receipt paper, scribbled, *This is my two weeks' notice. I quit,* and handed it to the SM.

It later emerged that Salty Jr. harbored resentment because she believed that despite not fulfilling the required criteria, she should have been considered for the assistant services manager position, given her longer tenure at the salon.

Another policy I introduced was monthly one-on-one check-ins with each stylist. These individual meetings were for tracking progress towards achieving their professional goals, providing a space to discuss concerns or challenges they might be facing, and exploring potential pathways for promotion to the next stylist level. These one-on-one sessions were crucial because some stylists hesitated to express themselves openly in group settings, often conforming to the majority opinion.

By meeting with them individually, I aimed to create a safe and comfortable space where they could voice their thoughts and concerns without fear of judgment or peer pressure. These check-ins also demonstrated my commitment to supporting each stylist individually. I wanted to show that my role wasn't just about enforcing policies; I was also there to mentor, guide, and advocate for their personal and professional growth within the company.

Given the challenging dynamic with Miss Salty Pants, I decided to have another manager present during our one-on-one sessions. This decision prevented her from twisting my words and encouraged constructive dialogue without risking conflict.

During one of the monthly check-in meetings, I reviewed a particular stylist's goals. I pointed out that despite her years of experience with the company, she had yet to attain the Elite Stylist level, which is the highest tier. I explained to her that I firmly believed she possessed the talent and capability to meet the requirements for the Elite level. However, the stylist informed me that she had no interest in attaining the next level because the sales goal was higher, and she was afraid of potentially losing her existing clientele due to the increase in her service prices. Unfortunately, I responded insensitively, stating, "You just don't want to work that hard."

An hour later, I found myself in a meeting with my manager and the stylist, who said my remark hurt her feelings. I sincerely apologized, clarifying that hurting her was never my intention. I reassured her that my goal was to encourage her to seize every opportunity for growth and maximize her potential within the company.

That experience taught me that not everyone has the same work ethic and goals as me, and that was okay. I also learned the importance of choosing my words carefully and approaching such discussions with empathy and an open mind rather than making assumptions or dismissive statements.

Three months into my position as the assistant services manager, I talked with a higher-up who suggested I focus on the stylists who wanted to grow their careers. I took her advice and adopted that approach, which was fruitful for three particular stylists. The first was a newly hired stylist I had brought to the team. Under my guidance and mentorship, she managed to level up and attain the next tier of stylist in less than a year. Not only did she rapidly advance her skills, but she also successfully built a solid clientele, laying a strong foundation for her blossoming career.

The second was also a new hire I brought to the team, but she had over fifteen years of experience in the industry. However, she had taken a hiatus from the profession to raise her children. Initially, it took her some time to readjust to the demands of the job, but with a little push and TLC, she quickly regained her confidence and speed.

The third stylist had been with the company for a few years but had yet to level up. By embracing my management style and taking advantage of the development opportunities offered, she gained the confidence to level up and unlock her true potential as a stylist. She thanked me for empowering her growth, which resulted in her earning more money than ever before.

By dedicating my time and efforts to providing these stylists with the necessary support, guidance, and gentle push they needed, I had the privilege of witnessing their remarkable growth and professional development unfold within a relatively short period of time. Fostering their talents and nurturing their skills was what I had set out to achieve as the assistant services manager. Watching them blossom, gain confidence, and ultimately thrive in their respective roles brought me so much joy.

Around the nine-month mark as the assistant services manager, the initial hostility and resistance from the team started to subside. Most of the stylists had accepted my role and were gradually adjusting to my management style. However, Miss Salty Pants still had an attitude and gave me pushback at every opportunity she could find. While her conduct remained a challenging aspect to navigate, her behavior fortunately did not affect the overall operations of the salon. Thanks to the team's collective efforts, our salon thrived and consistently achieved its goals.

"For we wrestle not against flesh and blood, but against principalities,
against powers, against the rulers of the darkness of this world,
against spiritual wickedness in high places."
(Ephesians 6:12, ESV Bible)

Chapter 8

Catalina, Conflicts, and Crazy Faith

During that strenuous yet rewarding period at work, Bryce and I were repairing our relationship. We had open conversations about setting boundaries and we shared our expectations with each other. I assured him I would not rush him, and he promised to communicate more effectively.

Progress was only possible because we were both willing to put in the effort, and I consistently attended therapy sessions. My therapist and I met once a week, and our discussions primarily centered around my relationship with Bryce. She provided step-by-step guidance and helped me navigate every thought and situation related to him. I disclosed everything to her because I wanted to make sure I didn't do anything to jeopardize my relationship with Bryce.

Through those sessions, I gained the insight that while I excelled as a leader in my professional life, I struggled in my personal relationships due to my tendency to seek control. She explained that relationships are like a dance, and I needed to allow the man to lead. If he took one step forward, I should mirror that with one step of my own. I was cautioned against moving faster than him or inadvertently overstepping boundaries, i.e., "stepping on his toes."

My life was truly flourishing, both professionally and personally. Despite Miss Salty Pants and her antics, I had the man I wanted and I had secured the assistant services manager position. A profound sense of fulfillment took over me as everything I had prayed for seemed to be falling into place.

With my 37th birthday approaching, I told Bryce I needed a vacation. We decided to take a mini getaway to Catalina Island. This island is located southwest of Los Angeles and is one of California's Channel Islands. It's renowned for its wildlife, dive sites, and Mt. Orizaba, its highest peak. The resort town of Two Harbors lies to the north, while the city of Avalon lies to the south. In Avalon, palm trees and cabanas line Descanso Beach. The city's iconic Catalina Casino, a circular Art Deco building, serves as a cultural center with a movie theater, ballroom, and museum.

We took a high-speed ferry to reach the island, which was about an hour from the mainland. The waters were so choppy during our ferry ride that several passengers became seasick. I won't lie; my stomach felt like it was doing somersaults, but I managed to keep it together.

Once we arrived on the island, we had to locate the golf cart rental office. Since the island is so small, most residents owned golf carts instead of cars. Bryce was excited to explore the island and partake in a few water sports. However, I made it very clear that I did not intend to do any of that. All I wanted was to lay on the beach and enjoy a couple of margaritas. He understood and said, "Well, it's your birthday, so you can do whatever you like."

Beaches, margaritas, and the love of my life by my side feeding me nachos—what more could a gal ask for on her birthday? My time in Catalina was amazing, even though it was just a day trip. The memories made were worth every second. Once again, I was swept up in the euphoria of love with Bryce. Everything was perfect, and I couldn't help but believe that the best was yet to come.

Two weeks after our trip, around the same time that Miss Salty Pants caused all that drama at work, Bryce and I had a conflict because of certain behaviors of his that I felt compelled to address. While I aim to be upfront about my feelings, Bryce seemed unaccustomed to that level of candor and accountability.

Initially, he appreciated my honesty and straightforward nature, saying he never had to guess where he stood with me. However, when I expressed my dislike for his actions so openly, it caused tensions. Although Bryce apologized, my direct approach didn't sit well with him; he wasn't used to being called out in that manner.

That week was one of the worst weeks of my life. On Tuesday, I was promoted to assistant services manager, which should have been an exciting milestone. However, on Wednesday, Miss Salty Pants began undermining my authority and creating drama. Things escalated on Thursday when Miss Salty Pants took her grievances to the human resources department, claiming unfair treatment from the management team. Additionally, my personal relationship with Bryce became strained after we had a huge argument when I confronted him about his behaviors.

To make matters worse, on Friday, Bryce broke up with me again! This simultaneous attack on both my professional and personal life was unprecedented for me. I had never felt such a strong spiritual attack before! I questioned why I faced such turmoil when I had done nothing wrong. Even after discussing everything with my therapist, she confirmed that I wasn't at fault in either situation.

After Bryce broke my heart for the second time, I was done with him! I had already given him a second chance, which was difficult enough, but he squandered it. That made me lose all hope in the situation. I convinced myself that I must have misunderstood God's plan because desiring a relationship with someone who wasn't ready and was unwilling to work on their issues couldn't be His will. Maybe it was my flesh misleading me.

A mutual friend of ours, Red, tried to persuade me to be more understanding, citing that Bryce was going through some personal issues. Red claimed Bryce was a good person at heart, but he just needed to work through some things.

However, I responded bluntly, "That sounds like a personal problem."

"You really put Bryce in the doghouse?" Red remarked.

"No, he's in a coffin!"

While I understood Red's attempt to advocate for Bryce, I had already crossed over into what I call "I don't care land." Once I reach that point of indifference, there is nothing anyone can say or do to reignite my concern. That's why I always advise people to address issues with me while I still care.

As I prepared to throw myself the biggest pity party ever, Holy Spirit guided me to the notes section of my iPhone. I have a folder titled "God Speaks," where I write down everything God communicates to me. While scrolling through the notes in that folder, I paused to read a note I had written two months earlier. It read:

> *You will go on a journey that you will not understand, but I will see you through it. Stay anchored.*
>
> *There are things that I haven't revealed to you yet. I am preparing you for such a time as this. I am who I am!*

Y'all will get married. It's going to be rough, but stay the course. I will sustain you. I will see you through. I will be there every step of the way, even when it feels like I'm not. Trust me. Lean on me. Believe me. Keep going. Your faith is going to be tested, but you will get through it.

Once I read that note, it was as if all the hurt and anger left my heart. Don't get it twisted. I didn't immediately run and call Bryce. Instead, I left the situation in the Lord's hands. I said, "God, I place everything concerning Bryce in Your hands. I have tried everything, and if it's meant to be, You will have to make it happen."

God assured me He would handle the situation, so I felt confident this was where He wanted me—stepping back and allowing Him to take control. However, my impatience, perspective, and timeline made me doubt what God had promised.

I prayed and gave the situation back to God whenever I felt doubt creeping in. I understood what God was telling me, but if I'm being sincere, I didn't believe it 100%. When asked about my relationship with Bryce, I would say, "Maybe I heard God wrong, or maybe it was my desires I allowed to lead me instead of God."

One night, I prayed and heard God say, "Don't downplay your faith to others. Believe what I have told you and stand firm on it. That's faith."

Even after God told me that, there were still times when I wanted to see some action, and God would say, "Be still and know that I am God. I am not a man that I should lie."

My best friend, Modesty, asked me if I would get back together with Bryce, and my first response was, "I don't even see how it's possible because I know him. He would never initiate the conversation, and I sure won't be saying anything to him."

After a moment, I said, "Honestly, I don't even know. Some days, I leave it in God's hands, and others, I feel defeated."

God woke me up out of my sleep that night and said, "I am the God of restoration. What I join together, no man can separate. Not even you." He also said, "You said you're not going back this time. But your word doesn't hit like My word. My word does not return void."

God just kept confirming over and over again what He had told me.

In December 2021, six months after our breakup, I was preparing to visit Transformation Church in Tulsa, Oklahoma. Every year, Pastor Mike Todd leads his church in giving a sacrificial gift, called the Crazy Faith Offering, to set the tone and heart posture of putting God first in their lives as they enter a new year. Pastor Mike and his congregation give this offering in faith, believing that as they give, God will do what may seem "crazy" in their lives and the lives of others. He invites people from all over the world to join him and his congregation for this event. Pastor Mike encourages them to come with specific expectations for what God will do and to take a moment to reflect on what God is asking them to trust Him with and have crazy faith for it. I had been participating in this event remotely since 2018, and 2021 was the year I decided to attend in person.

In 2020, I joined what they call "Belong Groups" at Transformation Church. These are virtual, small groups with people from all over the country who meet on a designated day to fellowship and discuss the sermon Pastor Mike preached the previous Sunday. Being in that group challenged me to grow my faith. It also provided a sisterhood and safe space to be vulnerable and share my faith journey with like-minded people.

The leader of the group suggested that I become a leader for the next semester. Initially, I said no because I didn't feel like I was fully saved yet. Don't judge me! I just didn't want to play in God's face like that. I expressed my concerns to her, and she told me to pray about it and see what the Lord said. Well, guess what? I became a Belong Group leader the following semester. It was an incredible and fulfilling experience to serve women and be a sounding board for each other while diving deeper into our faith. I connected with one particular woman in the group, Traniece, and we decided to meet in Tulsa to attend the Crazy Faith Offering together.

While sitting in the airport waiting to board my plane to Tulsa, I began talking to God, saying, "God, I know you'll blow my mind during this trip. Help me to be obedient to the things you tell and show me. Prepare my heart and mind and help me to have crazy faith."

After that, God told me to contact four people: my favorite aunt, Adrienne, my nephew Papa, Red, and Bryce. I sent a text that said,

> Good morning! I am about to board a plane to Tulsa to take my crazy faith offering to Transformation Church. I believe God is going to blow my mind and bless not only me but also the ones I love exceedingly, abundantly; above all that we can ask or think. Is there anything you want me to believe with you for?

Everyone texted me back with their requests except Bryce. He called to say he had just left the airport and then engaged in casual conversation. I was trying to remain focused and get the information I needed from him, but he was talking to me as if we were the best of friends, and I wasn't feeling it. So, I politely interrupted him, saying, "I'm sorry, but my plane is about to board. Text me your requests, and I'll let you know once I've filled out your crazy faith card."

Traniece and I arrived on a Saturday afternoon. After checking into our hotel and unpacking, we found a cozy Cajun restaurant across the street. Despite being our first in-person meeting, we clicked as if we'd been lifelong friends. We shared our life stories and expressed our excitement over what God had in store for us during this experience.

The next day, we watched the sermon online since the new church building was under construction, and they were using the old building for the Crazy Faith Experience. Our hotel room was filled with the spirit as we worshiped and prayed over our crazy faith requests, and God told me that He would do everything I put on my crazy faith card.

When we arrived at the Crazy Faith Experience later that evening, the line stretched around the building. Although we waited in line for at least an hour, it didn't feel that long because we made new friends, sang worship songs, and shared laughter with those around us. Everyone in line was pleasant, and the church staff was exceptional. They circulated through the crowd, ensuring everyone was comfortable, praying with a few individuals, and conducting interviews to capture people's experiences.

By the time we got inside, we were so full of expectation that we couldn't wait to pour out our praise before the Lord. The atmosphere felt like we were walking into the Holy of Holies (if you know, you know). The room was dimly lit, with designated areas for people to lie down, sit, or stand and tables were available for filling out crazy faith cards. Once the cards were completed, we placed them along the walls for the church staff to pray over at a later. Prayer partners were also available for anyone seeking personal prayer. It was such a beautiful and reverent experience.

Afterward, Traniece and I visited the Greenwood District, also called "Black Wall Street." Unfortunately, the Greenwood District was not as thriving as it once was due to the Tulsa Race Massacre. The Tulsa Race Massacre, also known as the Tulsa Race Riot or the Black Wall Street Massacre, was a two-day-long white supremacist terrorist attack that took place between May 31 and June 1, 1921. It devastated the once-prosperous African American community. Today, there is a museum located in that area dedicated to telling the history of this historic district and the tragic massacre that took place.

After a long day, I received a text from Bryce as I relaxed in my hotel room. It stated that his HR department had contacted him on a Sunday and asked if he was interested in a transfer to Arizona. He was in shock because, on his crazy faith card, he asked me to pray that God would clarify whether he should move, where to move, and his job situation.

I always knew you were one of God's favorite people, he said.

Wow, God is good. This trip has been amazing, and I love you, Bryce, I replied. *I love you too, Tavia, and thank you for all you do for me.*

The exchange highlighted the remarkable way God had answered Bryce's prayer for clarity, using the very trip and crazy faith offering as the vessel for His response. It was a powerful affirmation of faith and a testament to how God keeps his promises.

"Now faith is the substance of things hoped for,
the evidence of things not seen."

(Hebrews 11:1, ESV Bible)

Chapter 9

Harvest Season

When Bryce finally admitted his love for me, ya girl was on cloud 9! It was like time had slowed, and I felt warm and fuzzy. Deep down, I already knew, but his confirmation "sent me swingin'", in the words of Mint Condition. It was a moment that I'll never forget. He followed up with a text suggesting we go to dinner upon my return as a token of his appreciation. I eagerly accepted and promised to let him know when I returned to town.

The next day, as my flight touched down in California, I wasted no time contacting Bryce.

"When are you going to take me to dinner?"

His reply was prompt: "Tonight works if you're free."

"Perfect," I told him.

He requested that I pick a place, and I opted for the local gem, Le Papagayo. It was a vibrant eatery offering Mediterranean and coastal-inspired fare, outdoor dining, and nightly music.

After racing home from the airport, I peeled off my travel-worn clothes the moment I arrived. Refreshed by a steamy shower, I slipped into a pair of high-waisted jeans that hugged my curves and a cozy cropped sweater that bared a sliver of midriff. The casual-chic ensemble was cute yet comfortable—the perfect blend for an evening of rekindling.

As I entered the restaurant, I spotted Bryce seated at our table. His smooth milk chocolate skin seemed to glow in the soft lighting. With every step I took toward him, my heart raced faster, and my mind was completely captivated by how strikingly handsome he was.

While I was cute and casual, Bryce looked debonair in all black—black slacks, a black sweater, and a black peacoat. Since I was clearly underdressed, I demanded a redo date, which was also my way of securing another date. He insisted that I looked beautiful as always, but ya girl wanted to show him how I could really put on.

That evening at Le Papagayo, a rock cover band played the opening chords of "Wild Horses," which is my favorite song by the Rolling Stones. I turned to Bryce with an inviting smile and asked him to join me on the dance floor. As the beautiful music filled the air, we embraced and swayed to the rhythm, oblivious to the other diners present.

At that moment, we were the only two people in existence, lost in the magic of the music and the electricity between us. The memory of dancing with Bryce to one of my favorite songs will forever be etched into my heart.

The night held the promise of a new beginning for us both. A profound sense of certainty captured us—this was the right time, the destined moment. Though we had each grappled with resistance and denial, ultimately surrendering our wills to God finally allowed our relationship to blossom. With God as our guide, what was once constrained could now flourish uninhibited. Our hearts and souls were open to this budding relationship and ready to embark upon the next chapter together.

December of 2021 arrived like a long-awaited harvest season, a time of reaping what had been tenderly sown. All the seeds and tears I had planted had finally begun to bear fruit; a testament to perseverance. Each labor of love, every act of faith once cast into the fertile soil, now yielded a bountiful crop. The hard-won harvest ushered in an era of abundance, a sweet reward for the trials endured and the dreams tenaciously clung to. It was a season to rejoice in the nourishing bounty cultivated through unwavering belief.

This may sound odd or even unbelievable to you, but this is my truth, and if you can't tell by now, I keep it real!

Every January for the past few years, I've participated in 21 days of prayer and fasting organized by Transformation Church. They provided a structured outline to guide participants through the experience. Each evening during this time, they offered worship services, prayer sessions, and occasionally a brief sermon.

On January 19th, 2022, at 5:12 p.m., our topic was "Provision and Stewardship." As I was praying that evening, I felt the Lord instructing me to pray over my womb, conveying that it would carry my child. I also experienced a vivid image of Bryce holding and praying over our future child.

Two days later, on January 21st, 2002, at 6:04 a.m., the Lord again prompted me to lay my hands on my womb and pray for it to be blessed and fruitful. I also prayed for the protection of my unborn baby during this time. Another powerful vision of a hospital room came to me—I was lying in bed, and Bryce was walking around, cradling our newborn child with adoration and giving thanks to God.

Three days after the previous vision, on January 24th, 2022, at 5:22 a.m., I was worshiping the Lord when I had another vivid vision. In this one, I saw Bryce and myself—I was visibly pregnant, and he was kneeling on one knee, tenderly kissing my belly. During this vision, I distinctly heard God's voice saying, "I got you, Tavia. I am here with you."

This held particular significance because the theme for Transformation Church that year was "Here is Holy," meaning that wherever God had placed you in the present moment was sacred ground because of His presence there. It wasn't about a future point in time or dwelling on the past, but recognizing the holiness in your current circumstances through God's abiding presence.

Now, y'all, I already decided that I did not want another child, and when I met Bryce, he didn't want kids either. Furthermore, we were not married, and in the Christian faith, you are not supposed to have children out of wedlock. So, when I started receiving these vivid visions and explicit instructions from God about pregnancy and childbirth, I was perplexed. It seemed to contradict the convictions. Nevertheless, I obediently followed the divine prompting, praying as instructed, though I couldn't fully comprehend its meaning. Part of me even wondered if the visions weren't meant for me but were instead for Modesty, who had just discovered she was expecting.

Thirty-four days after that profound vision, a pivotal moment arrived that would forever alter the trajectory of our lives. I remember the details vividly, as if they had been etched into my memory just yesterday. My monthly cycle was four days late, and a strange, undeniable intuition stirred within me. With a mixture of trepidation and anticipation, I phoned Bryce to inform him that my cycle had not come.

He calmly said, "Okay," betraying none of the turbulence I imagined he must have felt.

I told Bryce I would wait a few more days, giving my cycle a chance to start before taking a pregnancy test. However, my nerves were frayed, and a knot of anxiety tightened in my stomach—I couldn't bear the suspense of waiting.

Throwing caution to the wind, I didn't even make it through that proposed waiting period. Instead, I went to the nearby CVS pharmacy and purchased not one, but two, pregnancy tests. I needed undeniable confirmation, one way or the other, and I needed it ASAP.

The pregnancy tests felt like they were burning a hole in my pocket as I rushed home. Peculiarly, my mom's cat followed me into the bathroom and sat right next to me as I prepared to take the life-altering test. The cat seemed to study me intently with wide, anxious eyes as if she understood the gravity of the moment. (As a sidebar, I mention the cat because, for some inexplicable reason, cats have held a significant presence throughout the pivotal junctures of my life's journey.)

With trembling hands, I finally mustered the courage to take the test. And there it was, those two fateful parallel lines materialized, confirming what I'd intrinsically known. I was undoubtedly pregnant. In that surreal moment, instinct took over. I did what any woman would do—I immediately called my best friend to share the monumental news.

For over twenty years, Modesty has been more than my best friend—she's my soul sister. We've weathered everything together since high school: celebrating our graduation from cosmetology school, grieving the losses of our children, supporting each other through job changes, and even surviving car accidents. And now, we would be pregnant together, traversing this next great life adventure side-by-side as we always had.

She was ecstatic! Me, not so much. I was a small group leader who had just started working in the teen ministry again, and many young girls and women looked up to me. This brought on a lot of guilt, shame, and anxiety. I knew better, I taught them better, and here I was, a Christian, pregnant and unmarried.

I knew I had to tell my church leaders, and I was apprehensive because, in my mind, I had let them down. After days of trying to figure out the right way to tell them and get out of my guilt and shame, I told them, and I was received with so much love and grace that I didn't know how to take it. As a matter of fact, I was perturbed that they weren't angry with me or warning me about eternal damnation for my behavior. They were God's grace and mercy personified.

I dreaded telling my small group the news because I knew how deeply it would affect them. I had led this group for about six months, and we had developed a strong bond. We all looked forward to our weekly meetings, where we encouraged, listened to, and supported one another. However, due to my sins, those meetings would now end. Your sins don't just affect you, now that'll preach, but I digress.

As their facilitator, I was supposed to lead by example and be above reproach. The thought of sharing this news face-to-face or over a video call felt overwhelming, so I sent a detailed text message to explain my situation and express my sincere apologies.

Again, I was met with overwhelming love and grace. Each group member reached out individually, calling or texting, to check my well-being and offer their unwavering support throughout my journey.

Despite their gracious reactions, I still felt stepping down from my leadership role was appropriate. My upbringing influenced this decision. In a Baptist church, leaders involved in scandalous behavior or sin were expected to step down temporarily. This practice allowed time for proper counseling and resolution of the issue.

Although my group members showed me nothing but love and acceptance, I believed this traditional approach was the right path forward for my growth and the group's integrity.

This unexpected pregnancy journey marked a profound turning point in my life. What began as a moment of fear and uncertainty transformed into a testament to God's unwavering faithfulness and the power of His plans. Despite my initial struggles with guilt and shame, I was met with an outpouring of love, grace, and support from those around me—a true reflection of God's mercy.

This experience taught me valuable lessons about judgment, forgiveness, and the unpredictable nature of God's timing. It reinforced the idea that our perceived mistakes or deviations from the "right" path can often lead us to exactly where we are meant to be.

My relationship with Bryce, the visions I received during prayer, and the surprising news of my pregnancy all wove together to create a tapestry of divine intervention. Though it didn't align with my original plans or societal expectations, this new path was a blessing in disguise.

"For I know the plans I have for you, declares the LORD,
plans for welfare and not for evil, to give you a future and a hope."

(Jeremiah 29:11, ESV Bible)

Chapter 10

Expecting and the Unexpected

Two weeks before learning of my pregnancy, Bryce had embarked on a new chapter in his own life, relocating to Texas for a promising job opportunity. This move was connected to the crazy faith card discussed in Chapter 8. On that card was a written prayer request asking God for guidance on three specific matters: whether Bryce should move, where he should move to, and what he should do about his job situation. Bryce's move to Texas appeared to be the answer to those prayers.

His new position was set to begin in the second week of February, coinciding with Valentine's Day. I planned to fly out the weekend before his Monday start date to celebrate Valentine's Day with him. To assist with the move, Bryce's dad flew in from Georgia to help him drive to Texas. They left on Wednesday to meet me at the airport on Friday.

During our time together in Texas, Bryce and I decided on the future of our relationship. We agreed to maintain a long-distance relationship for one year. At the end of that year, we planned to get married, after which I would relocate to Texas to join Bryce. Little did we know, things would not quite go as planned.

I discovered I was pregnant at approximately four weeks. Just four days after this revelation, I experienced bleeding and cramping, which led to an emergency room visit. Due to the potential risk of miscarriage, I required close monitoring. As a result, I had to return to the hospital three more times to check my human chorionic gonadotropin (HCG) levels. If the levels increased, then the pregnancy was progressing normally. If they decreased, that was an indication of complications.

The emergency room doctor informed me that my HCG levels were increasing, but not as quickly as expected. She recommended I follow up with my doctor for continued monitoring. This made me realize I hadn't yet decided on a healthcare provider to oversee my pregnancy and care for my unborn child.

Then I remembered Dr. Trujillo, who had been my obstetrician when I was pregnant with my son. I searched for her information and found out she was still practicing, with an office about 25 minutes from where I lived. I reached out to Dr. Trujillo, and to my pleasant surprise, she remembered me.

During my first appointment with Dr. Trujillo, she assured me that she and her team would provide excellent care for my baby and me throughout this pregnancy. Dr. Trujillo also informed me that the bleeding and cramping that I was experiencing was due to a subchorionic hemorrhage, which is bleeding beneath the chorion membranes that enclose the embryo in the uterus. She immediately referred me to a specialist to find out why this was occurring, and that's when I found out I had a short cervix—a term entirely new to me.

Because short cervixes are associated with preterm labor, Dr. Trujillo recommended that I remain off work for the entire duration of my pregnancy. After negotiating, I settled for working part-time. However, after just a couple of weeks of part-time work, I experienced further bleeding and ultimately heeded my doctor's advice to take complete rest.

Due to the complications and high-risk nature of my pregnancy, I had to visit the doctor every two weeks. During these prenatal checkups, nurses would attach monitor bands across my stomach. These bands were strapped across my belly like a seatbelt, tracking the baby's heart rate and movements for an hour. The monitoring machine also had a microphone to hear the baby's activity inside the womb. Sometimes, the sounds were so vigorous it seemed like the baby was rearranging furniture in there.

Dr. Trujillo prescribed progesterone to safeguard my pregnancy. I was instructed to administer the progesterone vaginally every night until I reached the 36th week of pregnancy. The purpose of this treatment was to reduce the risk of preterm labor, which could have posed risks to the baby's health.

During the second trimester of my pregnancy, I required weekly iron infusions for two months. These infusions were necessary to address my iron deficiency, which is not uncommon during pregnancy but can be severe if left untreated. In addition to the iron infusions, my doctor recommended another preventive measure, baby aspirin. This also helped to reduce the risk of preterm labor.

Due to the extensive testing and close monitoring required during my pregnancy, we had the opportunity to learn our baby's sex very early, at only 11 weeks. Since Bryce was living in Houston, I devised a plan to share this exciting discovery with him. I asked the nurse to seal the results of the baby's sex in an envelope. This way, Bryce and I could open it together during a FaceTime call, allowing us to experience this special moment simultaneously despite the distance between us.

Bryce was grinning from ear to ear before I could open the envelope.

"Why are you cheesing so hard?" I asked.

"Because I'm excited! Aren't you?" He replied.

"I am, but I already know it will be a boy."

"Oh really?!"

"Yup!"

"I don't care what the sex is. All I want is a healthy baby," Bryce said."

"Ready?" I asked

Before Bryce could respond, I ripped the envelope open and dramatically pulled the paper out. There, circled in bright yellow highlighter: "Sex—consistent with female." I was flabbergasted! Deep down, I had been so sure I was carrying a boy. While I wasn't disappointed, the news left me momentarily speechless. As the initial shock wore off, reality set in: I would have a little girl—a mini-me!

The pregnancy was taxing, both mentally and physically. Repeated hospital visits and the constant threat of losing the pregnancy caused me intense stress and anxiety. The psychological warfare raging in my mind was the most formidable adversary throughout this journey. The negative intrusive thoughts were relentless, and the paralyzing terror that threatened to engulf me was a constant, unwelcome companion.

What if I bleed out? What if I lose the baby? This is your punishment for getting pregnant out of wedlock.

These persistent, unwanted worries about the pregnancy's outcome were hard to control.

Despite my difficult pregnancy, I held onto my faith. I found comfort in believing God had assured me everything would turn out well. In fact, He had even revealed my pregnancy to me before I discovered it through conventional means. I trusted that God wouldn't lead me astray—that's not His nature. He is a faithful God, an on-time God, a way-maker, a miracle worker, and a promise-keeper! I admit there were moments when doubt and fear tried to take hold. When I tell you the Devil was busy—that mug was working overtime! But I reminded myself of God's consistent presence in my life. He has never disappointed me or let me down. I could go on and on, but I'll resist the urge to start preaching!

Dealing with these challenges without Bryce by my side was incredibly tough. Some days, all I craved was a simple hug from him. Despite the physical distance, Bryce made every effort to show his support. He sent gifts and flowers, and we FaceTimed several times each day. Once my doctor gave me the green light to travel, we took turns flying to see each other, bridging the gap as best we could.

I spent about five weeks in Texas on my last visit before our daughter was born. This visit coincided with both Bryce's birthday and Father's Day. I arranged a special 4D ultrasound appointment to celebrate Father's Day, allowing Bryce to see our baby girl for the first time.

At our ultrasound appointment, Bryce couldn't contain his excitement. The high-quality image on the screen provided a detailed view of our unborn baby girl. To our amazement, we could clearly see her facial features, which bore a striking resemblance to Bryce's. The similarity was so remarkable that even the experienced ultrasound technician commented on it, expressing surprise at how closely the baby's features matched her father's.

To celebrate Bryce's birthday, we decided to indulge in a special evening out. We began with a delectable dinner at The Oceanaire Seafood Room, an upscale restaurant known for its fresh, premium seafood. After dinner, our celebration continued as we went to a concert venue to see Keke Wyatt. Her powerful voice filled the room when she took the stage, treating us to a mix of soulful R&B classics and her hit songs. We sang along, swayed to the music, and lost ourselves in the moment. It was the perfect end to Bryce's birthday celebration.

At six months pregnant, I was thoroughly drained from the festivities on Friday and Saturday. That Sunday, I only wanted to relax at home and indulge in some snacks. However, Bryce informed me that his sister, who lived three hours away, wanted to meet me, and she had decided to make the drive to join us for brunch.

We met at Snooze, one of my favorite brunch spots in Houston. Bryce's sister, Janessa, was stunning with her rich chocolate skin, elegant sister locs, and a million-dollar smile. Her kind and sweet demeanor made an immediate impression. After we finished our meal, Bryce suggested that Janessa and I explore the shopping center while he ran a quick errand. Now, usually, I would have a ton of questions for Bryce.

"Where are you going?" "Why can't we go?" "How long are you going to be?"

But I had a pretty good idea of what he had up his sleeve, so I didn't question him.

About an hour into our exploration turned shopping spree, I asked Janessa what was taking her brother so long.

"I don't know, you know he's a little slow at doing things."

"Yeah, but I know what he's doing," I chuckled.

"You do?!"

"Yup."

"Wait, is this something you want?" She asked inquisitively.

"Yes!"

"Whew, I was going to say give me a code word, and I'll get you out of here!"

We fell out laughing.

Finally, Bryce called Janessa and told her to take me to an undisclosed location.

We arrived at a beautiful park in downtown Houston with a magnificent waterfall. As Janessa parked the car, Bryce walked up to greet us. He took me by the hand, and we walked towards the waterfall.

As we approached, I noticed mint green and pink balloons decorating the area.

Suddenly, Bryce began to pour his heart out. He told me how deeply he loved me, how profoundly I had impacted his life, and how being with me made him feel truly content and confident. As we reached the balloons, Bryce knelt on one knee. With trembling hands, he produced a small red box and opened it to reveal a breathtaking ring—a rose gold morganite surrounded by a floating halo of diamonds.

"Would you give me the honor of becoming my wife?" he asked, his voice filled with emotion.

"YES!!!" I exclaimed, overcome with joy.

To my surprise, a crowd had formed around us, and everyone was cheering. That moment couldn't have been any more perfect.

"Now to him who is able to do far more abundantly
than all that we ask or think, according to the power at work within us."
(Ephesians 3:20, ESV Bible)

Chapter 11

Anxious Anticipation

When I returned to California, I was seven months pregnant. Despite the numerous preventive measures making the pregnancy relatively smooth at this point, I couldn't shake my lingering anxiety about the outcome. My mind focused on one goal: surpassing the eight-month mark, even by a day. I believed reaching this point meant I would be in the clear.

This milestone was particularly significant for me because my son was stillborn when I was eight months pregnant. Given this history, you can likely understand the deep-seated fear I was battling. Each day brought me closer to that critical point, carrying both hope and dread. Some days, it felt like the sea of emotions would overtake me, but I knew the Lord would never put more on me than I could bear.

When I finally reached the eighth month, it was an emotional rollercoaster. Grief for my son crashed over me in waves while I was trying to cherish this new life growing inside of me. Simultaneously, anxiety about the myriad of complications gnawed at my consciousness while fervently praying for my baby's survival.

Bryce arrived a week before my scheduled C-section. In the days leading up to the big event, he dove headfirst into daddy duty, tackling my honey-do list of pre-baby preparations. His list consisted of assembling the bassinet, swing, changing table, and a plethora of other baby essentials. Watching Bryce meticulously assemble each item warmed my heart. It was a tender glimpse into the devoted father he was already becoming, even before our little one's arrival. As each piece came together, I saw the realization in his eyes that we were about to become parents.

Near the end of my pregnancy, I had doctor's appointments twice a week as another precaution. My last appointment was scheduled for the day before my planned C-section. I asked my doctor if this final check-up was necessary. She initially said no but then changed her mind, saying: "We've been cautious with your care plan throughout your pregnancy. I'd rather not take any chances now. It's better to be safe than sorry."

The day before our daughter's due date, we checked into a hotel near the hospital. We made this decision because my home was 30 minutes away. By staying closer, we ensured we could quickly reach the hospital in case of an emergency.

We then went to my last prenatal appointment. At the doctor's office, several of the staff members came to express their excitement and well wishes while we waited for the ultrasound technician. When she arrived, she asked,

"How are you feeling? Are you ready for the big day?" with a huge smile on her face.

"A little anxious, but I'm excited to see her little face."

The technician then asked, "What about you, dad?"

"I'm ready!" Bryce exclaimed.

As the ultrasound technician was performing the ultrasound, she asked me if my water had broken.

"No," I replied.

"Well, that's strange because your amniotic fluid a couple of days ago was 15 cm, and now it's 7 cm."

"Ya know, come to think of it, I did have a very long pee this morning."

"Hmmm, give me a sec." She responded and exited the room.

Y'all, don't judge me! I had no clue my water had broken. In my defense, I'd always been told to expect a dramatic gush, like a miniature Niagara Falls making an unexpected appearance. Instead, what I experienced felt more like an extended pit stop at the ladies' room.

After a few minutes, she returned to the room and asked,

"Do y'all have your hospital bags in the car?"

"No, they're at the hotel," I said.

"Hotel?!" she said, with a puzzled look.

"Yes, we wanted to be closer to the hospital."

"Oh, okay. Well, I spoke with the doctor on duty, and she thinks it's best that you all head over to the hospital now. Given the drastic decrease in your amniotic fluid, we think your water may have broken."

My heart was racing, and intrusive thoughts ricocheted through my mind like pinballs. Bryce could tell that I was worried. He came over to me, placed his hand on mine, and said, "Everything is going to be ok."

I exhaled and silently prayed to God:

You have not brought me this far in my pregnancy to leave me. You promised me everything would be okay, and I believe it because you are not a God who lies. I am scared. Guide me through this.

"We have already called the hospital, and they are waiting for you," the ultrasound technician said. She hugged me and sent us on our way.

Upon our arrival, we were swiftly escorted to our room. In a flurry of activity, the staff connected me to all the monitors; their beeps and hums constantly reminded me of the momentous occasion.

Then came the unexpected news: Dr. Trujillo was off duty, but she had personally requested Dr. Dumas to oversee my care. I had seen Dr. Dumas once previously when Dr. Trujillo was on vacation. However, this unexpected switch to Dr. Dumas before my delivery caused additional stress. Dr. Trujillo and I had carefully developed a birth plan together, and I had trusted her to deliver my baby girl safely.

As if sensing my mounting distress, Dr. Trujillo called me personally, expressing sincere regret about not being able to deliver my daughter. She assured me I was in capable hands with Dr. Dumas because she had delivered her children. Dr. Trujillo promised to monitor my progress remotely and said I could call her if needed. Her thoughtful call demonstrated that she cared about me as more than just a patient, which helped ease my nerves somewhat.

Dr. Dumas came in to inform us that we would have a bit of a wait because they had a couple of patients with more urgent needs than me. She told me they would still be monitoring me closely and would let us know if there were any changes.

After an agonizing seven-hour wait, the nurses finally arrived to prepare me for surgery. Bryce, overflowing with anticipation, eagerly captured every moment on camera. Meanwhile, my anxiety intensified with each passing second.

Throughout my pregnancy, I never once worried about myself, even though I had experienced severe hemorrhaging with my son, requiring a blood transfusion during my emergency C-section. My singular goal in this procedure was for my baby girl to be born alive and well.

As the medical team prepared me for the C-section, I noticed they were engaging in a lot of chit-chat. They discussed lunch plans and hospital gossip while preparing for the procedure. This casual atmosphere made me uneasy. Though I knew they were trying to keep things relaxed, I worried about their focus. This wasn't just any surgery—it was the birth of my child! I tried to calm myself by trusting their expertise. But I still felt less talking and more concentration would have been better for such a critical moment.

The anesthesiologist came over to explain the epidural process. He told me it would numb me from below my breasts to my toes and that I'd be awake but pain-free during the procedure. He warned that I might feel intense pressure during delivery, describing it as feeling like "an elephant sitting on your chest." He also mentioned that a curtain would separate my fiancé and me from the surgical team, preventing us from seeing the operation.

As he was administering the epidural, I heard him say, "Ohhhh, too high."

And what does that mean?! I thought to myself.

Well, I'll tell you what it meant. It meant that I couldn't feel a thing once the medication set in, and an eerie numbness crept through my entire body. My eyeballs were numb, and I couldn't speak. The anesthesiologist was right—it really felt like an elephant was sitting on my chest. I felt trapped in my own body, unable to tell anyone what I was experiencing. In that moment of helplessness, I forced myself to focus on steady, calming thoughts. *Don't freak out,* I silently chanted, reminding myself that any distress might affect the baby or complicate the procedure.

After what felt like an eternity, Munroe Nicole-Rene entered the world at 7:49 p.m., a petite bundle of joy weighing 6 pounds 8 ounces and 18 1/4 inches long. The nurses gently placed her on my chest, this tiny miracle warm against my skin, but I couldn't say anything. I couldn't cry or show any emotion because of the effects of the epidural. All I could manage to do was softly caress her perfect little face.

"The LORD himself goes before you and will be with you;
he will never leave you nor forsake you.
Do not be afraid; do not be discouraged."
(Deuteronomy 31:8, ESV Bible)

Chapter 12

A Beautiful New Beginning

This C-section experience was vastly different from my previous one. When I had my son, I only needed to focus on healing physically. This time, I had to recover while caring for a newborn, not to mention I was no spring chicken. I was 23 when I had my son but 38 when I had my daughter, making the recovery more challenging.

I realize now that the overwhelming grief from losing my son may have overshadowed my memory of the physical pain from that C-section. The pain I experienced this time was excruciating. Simple tasks like getting in and out of the hospital bed to use the bathroom felt torturous, and I would cry each time I needed to move.

Our first night with Munroe was challenging. She needed to be fed every 1.5-2 hours but had difficulty latching properly. Instead of taking the entire nipple in her mouth, she would only suck on the tip, causing extreme pain. I required the nurse's assistance with her latch for almost every feeding.

Sleep was impossible. Between Munroe's frequent feedings, my compulsive checking of her breathing, and the seemingly constant nurse visits, I remained awake all night. What caught me off guard were the intensified intrusive thoughts after giving birth—something no one had prepared me for. *What if the bassinet tips over? What if someone sneaks in and takes her while I'm asleep? What if she stops breathing? These thoughts plagued me incessantly.*

The following day, my mom and Papa visited us in the hospital. Papa was eager to hold Munroe. He gazed at her with the pride of a big brother-cousin as he held her. My mom, overcome with joy, couldn't tear her eyes away from her precious new granddaughter. Her face radiated with the particular kind of love only grandmothers seem to possess. Their adoration of little Munroe was interrupted by a nurse arriving to conduct the newborn screening. As she began preparing her equipment, my mom and Papa took that as their cue to say their goodbyes.

The nurse explained that this was a blood test for disorders not immediately apparent after birth. The test involved pricking Munroe's heel to collect a few drops of blood on a special paper, nothing too crazy. However, when the nurse began, she grabbed Munroe's foot rather aggressively, causing her to cry out. Instantly, the mama bear in me rose up.

"Do you have to grab her foot like that?!" I asked sharply.

Bryce tried to calm me, saying, "It's okay, babe. She's just doing her job."

"Well, I don't like how she's doing it," I retorted.

The nurse explained, "Ma'am, I have to hold her foot firmly so she doesn't kick while I squeeze the blood onto the paper."

"Breathe, Tavia," I whispered to myself.

When the nurse pricked Munroe's heel, my baby screamed in pain. I couldn't bear it and immediately tried to get up.

"Babe! You can't get up like that!" Bryce warned.

"I'm getting my baby!" I said sternly.

The nurse interjected, "Ma'am, I need to prick her heel again for a few more drops."

"Absolutely not!" I shouted.

Bryce tried reasoning, "Babe, you've got to let her do her job."

"The hell I do! She should have done it correctly the first time!"

By now, I was furious. The nurse stood silently as Bryce and I argued about her. Despite the pain, I got out of bed, picked up Munroe, and told the nurse she was done.

"Ma'am, I have to finish the procedure," the nurse insisted.

I firmly responded, "No, you don't. She's my child, and I said you're done! You'll have to find a way to work with what you've already collected."

Overwhelmed with emotion, tears streamed down my face. The intensity of my protective instinct surprised even me—I was determined to shield my baby from any harm, no matter who caused it.

Soon after, another nurse entered the room, likely informed by her colleague about the incident. Speaking gently, she explained that my recent childbirth had left my emotions and hormones in turmoil. She also noted my lack of proper rest, suggesting this might have intensified my reaction. While I understood her reasoning, I still disliked how that lady manhandled my baby.

After three days in the hospital, it was time to bring our newborn home. This prospect made me anxious. Half-joking, I asked the nurse if we could leave the baby at the hospital and visit daily. She laughed and reassured me, "You'll be fine, dear. It's normal to feel nervous about taking your baby home. Don't worry; your maternal instincts will guide you."

Boy, did I hope she was right. Fortunately, I found comfort in knowing I wouldn't be alone. Bryce stayed with us until January, and my mom was still at home, even though she was preparing to move to Las Vegas. Their presence eased my anxiety about caring for the baby on my own.

Settling into our new normal was exhausting, but Bryce and I developed a good routine. When the baby woke at night, I would feed her, and then he would change her and put her back to sleep if she wasn't still hungry. Some nights, she would wake up every hour on the hour to feed. These relentless nights left both of us in a fog of sleep deprivation, stumbling through our days on sheer willpower and caffeine.

Caring for a newborn while trying to maintain my mental health was a challenge that's rarely discussed. There were days when I wasn't sure who cried more—Munroe or me. I remember telling my mom that I wanted to write a letter to the women's counsel because I felt unprepared as a mother, and it was their fault for not telling me what to expect. I know there is no such thing, but somebody needed to be held accountable!

Thank God for Dr. Trujillo, who consistently checked and asked tough questions about my mental health. I never truly understood how the postpartum period could affect a woman until I experienced it firsthand. Despite help from my fiancé and family, there were days when I felt isolated and overwhelmed. Sometimes, I even wanted to run away because it all seemed too much to handle.

Despite having a newborn on our hands, Bryce and I decided to get married before he returned to Houston. This gave us only two months to plan our wedding. We opted for a small, intimate ceremony with our closest friends and family.

Our friends, Natrese and Red, generously offered their beautiful California home to serve as our venue. Their picturesque backyard provided the perfect setting for our special day. Natrese stepped up to be our wedding coordinator, while Red, an ordained minister, agreed to officiate the ceremony.

Bryce and I love exceptional food and music, so we made those the focal points of our wedding celebration. These elements would create the joyful, festive atmosphere we desired for our special day. My priority was booking the band, B.I.G—the same talented group I mentioned in Chapter 6. They were thrilled to be part of our celebration, which set the perfect tone for the event.

We were fortunate to have Natrese's cousin, a professional caterer, create a menu tailored to our tastes to ensure our guests would enjoy a memorable culinary experience. With the music and food arranged, our remaining tasks were straightforward: compile our guest list and select the decor. These final touches would complete our vision for an intimate and lively wedding celebration.

On January 7th, 2023, I experienced one of the happiest days of my life. The journey to this moment involved many challenges, including tears and difficult conversations, but these experiences ultimately prepared us for our walk down the aisle.

Our venue was stunning, adorned with an elegant palette of deep navy blue, lustrous gold, and crisp white. Natrese, with her impeccable attention to detail, had transformed my vision into a breathtaking reality. The ceremony space featured a beautiful white floral arch where we would exchange our vows. Our sweetheart table was adorned with sparkling decorations, creating a glamorous focal point. Each guest table was elegantly decorated with floral arrangements and tall vases with floating white, blue, and gold rose petals, adding a touch of magic to the decor.

As beautiful as the decor was, it had nothing on Bryce. He made his grand entrance looking very debonair in his navy-blue tux, holding our beautiful baby girl. The timeless melody of Stevie Wonder's "As" filled the air, setting a romantic tone for the ceremony. My nephews, playing their part perfectly, rolled out the pristine white carpet, creating a path for my grand entrance. My niece, the flower girl, scattered a trail of blue, white, and gold rose petals, adding a touch of elegance to the scene.

Jamie and Keith, my beloved fathers, proudly escorted me down the aisle as Jill Scott's soulful "He Loves Me" serenaded our procession. I couldn't help but feel radiant in my carefully chosen gown—a mermaid-style masterpiece that seemed designed just for me. The dress featured an exquisite lace-embroidered bodice with a sweetheart neckline adorned with shimmering gold jewels that caught the light with every step. The gown transitioned into smooth white satin from the hips down, culminating in a cascade of elegant ruffles from the knee to the floor. From the moment I first laid eyes on it, I knew this dress was destined to be mine for this special day.

As I reached the end of the aisle, my eyes met Bryce's, and in that moment, I felt the presence of God. We exchanged our vows with heartfelt "I dos", sealed our commitment with a tender kiss, and joyfully leaped over the broom, honoring tradition.

Red's voice rang out, clear and jubilant: "I present to you, Mr. and Mrs. Bradford!"

Those simple yet powerful words echoed through the air, seeming to crystallize God's promises. At that moment, our union felt celebrated and truly consecrated—a testament to faith, love, and the beautiful journey ahead.

A week after our wedding, Bryce returned to Houston to begin the search for our new home, as his one-bedroom apartment couldn't accommodate our shared life. In April, he found the perfect place—a brand-new home where we could build our future together.

Thirty days later, he flew to California to escort us to our forever home in Houston, Texas. There, we began our version of "happily ever after"—not a fairy tale, but a real-life adventure filled with love, laughter, and the occasional challenge.

Reflecting on my life, I see God's hand guiding me through every challenge. The enemy's tactics are to kill, steal, and destroy. He tried to kill me on several occasions. He tried to steal my joy and destroy my peace, but God protected me. What the enemy meant for evil, God turned into good. By God's grace, I endured. I have been blessed beyond measure and have a fantastic testimony of God's faithfulness, protection, and provision. No matter what I faced, God gave me beauty for ashes, the oil of joy for mourning. I am overflowing with gratitude for God's goodness. Like the old saints said, "As I look back over my life and think things over, I can truly say that I am blessed. I have a testimony!"

"Being confident of this, that he who began a good
work in you will bring it to completion until the day of Jesus Christ."
(Philippians 1:6, ESV Bible)

About the Author

Tavia Bradford's journey from the beaches of Oceanside, California, to the suburbs of Katy, Texas, is as colorful as her makeup palette; bringing a little West Coast flair to the Lone Star State.

She is a veteran hairstylist and makeup artist with over 20 years of experience. The work of her skilled hands has graced the pages of Essence magazine, film sets, and various faces across the country.

Over the course of her career, Tavia has had the privilege of working closely with Lisa Nichols in various capacities. Tavia began as Lisa's makeup artist and progressively expanded the role to include hair and wardrobe styling. Her expertise and dedication ultimately made her an integral part of Lisa's executive team. Tavia's talents have appeared in Lisa's magazine features, a book cover, The Lisa Nichols Show, and other television appearances.

Tavia's impact extends beyond the glitz and glam of magazines and film sets. As a former lay counselor at Birth Choice, she offered compassionate support to women facing difficult decisions.

With an Associate's degree in cosmetology from Mira Costa Community College, Tavia has transformed her passion into a multifaceted career. She's a former business owner who founded Z.J.E Hair Care and Meraki Beauty Lounge, demonstrating her entrepreneurial spirit.

She is also a facilitator for Measure, a company that provides free data support to powerful Black, Indigenous, and Brown-led organizations. Additionally, Tavia has served as a small group leader and director of operations for a small church plant, where she honed her leadership and organizational skills.

Tavia is an accomplished author whose memoir, "Blessings In The Chaos," tells of her journey through life's most daunting challenges and exhilarating victories. With raw honesty and profound insight, she illustrates how the twin forces of unconditional love and unshakable faith can not only sustain us through turbulent times but also catalyze remarkable personal transformation.

Tavia has left her mark on both the beauty industry and the lives of those she's touched. Her story is one of discovery, continuous growth and reinvention. She's not just a cosmetologist; she's a storyteller who uses her skills to edify, empower, and educate.

Props
aka
Acknowledgments

First, giving honor to God who is the head of my life! I've always wanted to say that. IYKYK!

God, I'm amazed that you love me despite my flaws. I'm often disobedient, stubborn, spoiled, and perhaps a bit crazy. But I'm deeply grateful for your love. This book only exists because of You. I don't even like to read, so the fact that I've written a book is clearly Your doing. You deserve all the glory for this accomplishment.

They say to give people their flowers while they can still smell them, so here is my heartfelt expression of love, gratitude, and appreciation to those who made this memoir possible.

Book Squad: This victory isn't mine alone; it belongs to all of us. You've dedicated months of your lives to this journey, offering your time, insights, and emotions. You've read tirelessly, critiqued thoughtfully, and supported me, and each other, with unwavering compassion. When I sought companions for this endeavor, I hoped for individuals who would challenge me, not simply agree. You've exceeded those expectations; providing the honesty and authenticity I needed to complete this work.

Each of you has carved out a unique place in my heart. Your friendship is a treasure I hold dear. Please know that my gratitude and love for you all runs deep and true.

My BFF: My ride-or-die, my sister from another mister, my confidante! Thank you for always being there with no judgment. Your friendship is a rare gift, one I truly cherish. I couldn't imagine navigating this journey without you by my side. You know I love you real bad.

My lovely little sisters: Words cannot fully express how proud I am of y'all and each one of you holds a special place in my heart. Know that my love and support for you and your children know no bounds and I would move mountains if you asked. I know I can be hard on y'all at times but please understand that it stems from a place of deep care and hope. My greatest wish is to see you lead lives brimming with purpose, joy, and fulfillment. You deserve nothing less! I love y'all.

Lisa Nichols: Thank you for pulling out a version of me that I didn't know existed and gently pushing me toward the greatness you saw in me. I will always cherish our talks and your guidance. Thank you for how you show up in the world, I love you!

Denise Nicholson (Bold Publishing): Thank you for sharing your invaluable knowledge, guidance, and expertise. Your support transformed my manuscript from mere words on a screen to a cherished work held in the hands of many.

My beautiful baby girl: You are the beating heart of my world, the living legacy I cherish, and the most profound blessing in my life. Your very existence fills me with wonder and joy. As you grow, I promise to nurture your dreams, celebrate your uniqueness, and strive to be the mother you deserve. You inspire me to be better every day.

My man, my man, my man; AKA my husband: I owe a debt of gratitude that words cannot explain. Throughout this challenging journey of penning my memoir, you've been my rock, my cheerleader, and my sanctuary. Your patience knew no bounds as I spent countless hours lost in memories and words. You listened tirelessly, offered insights, and held space for my emotions as I revisited both joyous and painful chapters of my life. Your love provided the safety net I needed to dive deep into my past, while your encouragement propelled me forward when self-doubt crept in. You celebrated every small victory and comforted me through every setback. This book is as much a product of your support as it is of my efforts. Thank you for believing in me, for sacrificing our time together, and for loving me through every page of this process. Your faith in me and in our love story has made this memoir possible.

www.ingramcontent.com/pod-product-compliance
Lightning Source LLC
Chambersburg PA
CBHW051532120626
46551CB00012B/1183